Explore! Joshua Tree National Park

Help Us Keep This Guide Up to Date

Every effort has been made by the author and editors to make this guide as accurate and useful as possible. However, many things can change after a guide is published—trails are rerouted, regulations change, techniques evolve, facilities come under new management, etc.

We would love to hear from you concerning your experiences with this guide and how you feel it could be improved and kept up to date. While we may not be able to respond to all comments and suggestions, we'll take them to heart and we'll also make certain to share them with the author. Please send your comments and suggestions to the following address:

The Globe Pequot Press
Reader Response/Editorial Department
P.O. Box 480
Guilford, CT 06437

Or you may e-mail us at:

editorial@GlobePequot.com

Thanks for your input, and happy trails!

A **FALCON** GUIDE®

Exploring Series

Explore! Joshua Tree National Park

Bruce Grubbs

FALCON GUIDE®

GUILFORD, CONNECTICUT
HELENA, MONTANA

AN IMPRINT OF THE GLOBE PEQUOT PRESS

A FALCON GUIDE®

Photos by Bruce Grubbs
Maps by Bruce Grubbs © Morris Book Publishing, LLC

Library of Congress Cataloging-in-Publication Data
Grubbs, Bruce (Bruce O.)
   Explore! Joshua Tree National Park : a guide to exploring the great outdoors / Bruce Grubbs. — 1st ed.
      p. cm. — (Exploring series) (A Falcon guide)
   Includes index.
   ISBN-13: 978-0-7627-3543-3
   ISBN-10: 0-7627-3543-0
   1. Joshua Tree National Park (Calif.)—Guidebooks. 2. Outdoor recreation—California—Joshua Tree National Park—Guidebooks. I. Title.
   F868.J6G78 2007
   917.94'970454—dc22

                                        2006026211

Manufactured in the United States of America
First Edition/First Printing

Contents

Acknowledgments

I appreciate the helpful comments made by Ken Hornback, trails supervisor at Joshua Tree National Park. Thanks also to my editors at the Globe Pequot Press, Bill Schneider and John Burbidge. And warm thanks to Duart, who supported this project every step of the way.

Two deserts meet in the mountains and valleys of southeastern California. The hot, low-elevation Sonoran Desert sweeps up to the west from the Colorado River and transitions to the cooler, high Mojave Desert along the Little San Bernadino Mountains. This unique desert area is protected within Joshua Tree National Park and Big Morongo Canyon Preserve. The region's blend of vast landscapes, wilderness, picturesque rock formations, wildlife, and desert plants attract millions of visitors each year. They come to hike, mountain-bike, rock-climb, camp, picnic, drive the scenic roads, and look for desert flowers.

This FalconGuide offers a complete overview of Joshua Tree National Park for the aspiring desert explorer. It will tell you how to get to the park and preserve and how to find the visitor centers, nature trails, picnic areas, campgrounds, and trails. The book features a guide to the trails of both the park and the preserve, as well as detailed descriptions of the natural and human history of the region.

Joshua Tree National Park is named for the Joshua tree, a giant yucca that grows up to 30 feet tall in the western Mojave Desert portion of the park. The lower eastern portion of the park is dominated by creosote bushes, which favor the lower, warmer Sonoran Desert. Scattered throughout the park are five California-fan-palm oases, where underground water rises to the surface to create islands of shade and greenery in the otherwise stark desert. Elevations in the park range from less than 1,000 feet above sea level at the southeast corner of the park to more than 5,800 feet at the highest peaks in the western sections. Exposed granite domes and twisted metamorphic

Upper Covington Flats has some of the largest Joshua trees in the park.

rocks not only create dramatic scenery but also show the power of natural forces. Desert features such as washes, dried lake beds, alluvial fans, bajadas, and pediments shape the landscape. Despite its barren appearance, the desert teems with life, all adapted to life in an arid, hot climate. Plants patiently endure long dry periods, waiting for seasonal rains to nuture spurts of growth. Animals wait out the heat and glare of day in cool burrows, then emerge during twilight and night to forage on the desert floor. The visitor who takes the time to observe the desert closely will discover its amazing variety, where life forms a complex mosaic that has survived for eons.

Zero Impact

Being close to the large population centers of southern California, Joshua Tree National Park is heavily used. The backcountry can handle a lot more people if they work to minimize their impact. Most backcountry users probably don't intentionally abuse the land, thinking that cutting switchbacks on trails, dropping orange peels, building campfires, trying to burn their trash, picking flowers and disturbing artifacts don't matter. But they do. Multiply each little impact by thousands of visitors, and soon the wild places look beaten down and hammered. Each visitor owes it to the thousands that will follow to have as close to zero impact as possible.

Three Falcon Principles of Zero Impact

Leave with everything you brought in.
Leave no sign of your visit.
Leave the landscape as you found it.

Most of us know better than to litter, but how many people think of orange peels as litter? In the desert climate, even organic litter such as orange and banana peels takes a long time to degrade. Tiny pieces of foil or paper from food wrappers may not seem like much, but they last for dozens of years and soon give the ground that littered, overused look. Likewise with cigarette butts. Consider picking up other people's litter on your way out. It adds little to your load while garnering a great deal of self-satisfaction.

Stay on the trail. Cutting switchbacks actually costs more energy than it saves and leads to erosion and loss of vegetation. Most trail work is done by volunteers since land-management agencies can no longer pay for trail maintenance. By cutting switchbacks, you're just creating more work for a fellow hiker who's given up some of her hiking time to keep your trails in good shape.

Don't ever pick flowers or disturb artifacts, historical objects, or any natural features. The next visitors want to see these things too. In the national park it's illegal to disturb or remove any natural feature, and federal law protects both

historic and prehistoric artifacts on all federal land. Report any such distur-
bance to the nearest ranger station or visitor center.

Avoid making loud noises on the trail or camp. You may be having a good
time, but don't ruin other people's backcountry experience. If you have a dog
with you, don't allow it to bark, especially in camp. Do not leave your dog in a
car or tied up unattended.

Remember that dogs are not allowed on trails in the national park and must
be on a leash on roads and in campgrounds. This rule protects wildlife from
stress and harassment, as well as protecting your dog. Remember that every
unpleasant dog-human encounter increases the number of places closed to dogs.

When nature calls, use public restrooms at visitor centers, campgrounds, or
trailheads whenever possible. If these facilities are present, it means that human
use of the area is too great for natural disposal systems.

In the backcountry, relieve yourself at least 200 feet from springs and creeks
and away from dry drainages and washes. Even if surface water is not present,
water is usually not far below the surface, and many usually dry streams do flow
for part of the year. To take advantage of the natural, biological disposal-system
present in soil, find a site in organic rather than sandy soil, if possible. Dig a cat
hole about 6 to 8 inches deep, staying within the organic layer of the soil. Carefully cover the hole afterward. Some hikers carry a plastic trowel for this purpose. Pack out all used toilet paper and personal hygiene items in double plastic
bags. Never burn toilet paper—numerous wildfires have been started this way.

Keep all camp waste, including toothpaste, dishwater, and soap, at least 200
feet from water. Never wash yourself or dishes in a spring or stream. Water is
rare in this desert environment and all too easily contaminated. Rock tanks, also
known as tinajas, are especially fragile and easy to contaminate. Remember that
many other people will need the same water sources and that wildlife depend
on them.

Camping in Joshua Tree National Park is allowed at vehicle campgrounds
and in the backcountry. Backpackers must register at one of the backcountry
boards located at trailheads throughout the park. (Day hikers do not need to
register.) Backcountry camps must be at least 1 mile from roads and 500 feet
from trails. Camping is prohibited in washes (due to the possibility of flash
floods) and in designated day-use areas. The trail descriptions in this book
mention whether all or part of a hike is in a day-use area. Restricted areas are
closed to all entry. There are no backcountry boards in the remote northeast-
ern portion of the park; backpackers wishing to explore this area should check
with rangers at the Cottonwood or Oasis Visitor Centers.

Campfires are not permitted in the backcountry, and backpackers should
plan on cooking on a stove. In campgrounds, campers must bring their own
wood from outside the park. Wood gathering is not allowed in the park.

Joshua Tree National Park charges an entrance fee, which is good for seven days. You can also purchase an annual pass for Joshua Tree National Park, a National Parks Pass good at all national parks and monuments, or a Golden Eagle Pass valid for all federal lands, including national parks and monuments, as well as U.S. Forest Service and Bureau of Land Management lands.

Strictly follow the pack-in/pack-out rule. Whether you're vehicle camping, day hiking, rock climbing, mountain biking, or backpacking, if you carried it in, you can and should carry it out.

Make It a Safe Trip

Although all the park is close to populated areas on the north and west sides, the eastern portion of the park is remote. Due to the rugged terrain, you can quickly find yourself in isolated backcountry anywhere in the park. While the Joshua Tree backcountry is as safe as any other, being prepared greatly increases your safety and that of your party.

Being prepared for a hike, rock climb, or bike ride requires more than just filling your hydration bladder and blasting off. Give a little thought to what could happen. Changes in the weather, an injury such as a sprained ankle, losing the trail, or overestimating your party's abilities can turn an easy outing into a scary epic.

Know your limitations. Be realistic about your level of physical and mental fitness for a given backcountry trek. Allow plenty of time so you won't be stressed out trying to reach camp or trailhead as the sun sinks to the horizon. Be willing to turn back if the outing is taking too long or a member of the group is having difficulty.

Check the weather forecast. In these desert mountains, an unusually hot spell can be as dangerous as an unexpected winter snowstorm. Late summer brings frequent thunderstorms with lightning, hail, and sudden heavy rain. Plan to be off high ridges and peaks by midday during thunderstorm weather, and never camp or leave a vehicle in a dry wash any time of year. Winter brings rainstorms to the desert and snow to the highest peaks. Occasionally, winter storms may drop snow at the lowest elevations of the park.

Avoid traveling alone unless you are fit and experienced, and then always leave a detailed trip plan and your time of return with a reliable person who knows whom to call if you don't return on time. A trip plan is also a good idea with a group. Even if you're confident the group can handle an injury or problem, it's always comforting to know that help will come. I prefer leaving a copy of my map with the route and any planned campsites marked, as well as the location and description of my vehicle and license number.

Learn first aid and basic survival skills in advance.

Don't eat wild plants unless you know what you are doing and then only in an emergency.

Before you leave the trailhead, study the maps and learn as much as you can about the route. Plan your outing and know what time you have to turn back or be at the halfway point in order to return to the trailhead or reach a good campsite or spring before dark.

Keep track of your progress on your map, even if you're on an easy trail. That way you can never become lost. You also know whether you are making reasonable progress toward your goal.

Don't exhaust yourself or members of your party by traveling too fast. A group should move at the speed of its slowest member. Faster hikers can take advantage of the leisurely pace to

Joshua trees have masses of cream-colored flowers.

look around or even explore side hikes. If anyone expresses reservations about the trail, route, ride, or climb, back off. And take plenty of rest breaks. Remember, you're out there to have fun, not to prove anything.

If you do get confused about your location, stop, sit down, have some water and munchies, and think about it. Chances are all you'll have to do is backtrack a bit to find the trail. Note your present location, then scout back along the way you came, looking for the trail or trail markers. Leave someone at the point where you lost the trail as a reference point, and stay within sight or at least earshot of that person. If you can't find the trail by backtracking, scout around your reference point in expanding circles. Have a look at your map and see if you can determine where the trail went. Never set off blindly cross-country without the trail, unless you are experienced and willing to commit to a cross-country hike. You can quickly find yourself in extremely rough country, where progress may be slow or impossible. The old saw about following a stream downhill to civilization will work in Joshua Tree, but it may take days to reach the nearest road or town. In addition, the weather gets hotter and drier at lower elevations, especially during the summer.

In the rare case of getting completely lost or being stranded because of injury, storm, or nightfall, stay put, provide shelter for the victim and the rest of the party, and plan on sending two people for help as soon as it's safe to do so. Never leave an injured person alone, even in parties of two. Signal for help instead.

If you have a cell phone, try it, but don't count on it working. While you may get a signal on high terrain, deep in the canyons you won't. Be familiar with the traditional methods of signaling for help. Three of anything—three shouts, blasts on a whistle, three columns of smoke or three fires, or three flashes of light—is the international distress signal. Mirror flashes are especially effective in sunny weather, when they can be seen for 100 miles. Practice with a signal mirror ahead of time, following the instructions that came with the mirror. The general technique is to sight through the sighting hole at your target, then move the mirror until there's a bright spot of sunlight on your target. This indicates that you're reflecting the sun directly at your target. Now, tap the mirror lightly to set up a flashing, twinkling appearance to the reflected sunlight so you'll catch the observer's eye. If the sun is low behind you, have someone stand in front of you with a second mirror and reflect the sun into your signal mirror. Signal mirrors are especially good for signaling aircraft.

Carry a basic first-aid, repair, and survival kit, containing at least the following: adhesive bandages, medical tape, gauze pads, a role of gauze, antiseptic ointment, moleskin, snakebite kit, sewing needle and thread, compass, whistle, signal mirror, flashlight or headlamp, lighter or other fire starter, water purification tables, a space rescue blanket, and a small booklet of first-aid and survival instructions. You should be able to treat minor injuries, such as cuts or scrapes and blisters, and stabilize victims of more serious injuries, as well as repair common problems with your gear, such as failed stitches, broken buckles or straps, tears in pack fabric, and missing parts such as clevis pins.

Avoid all wild animals. Feeding animals causes them to become dependent on human food and lose their natural fear of humans, which could lead to a dangerous future encounter and result in the destruction of the animal. Any mammal can carry rabies. See the "Animal Hazards" section for more information.

Weather

Although Joshua Tree is a desert park, the highest elevations can experience significant snowfall from December through March, and occasionally even in October and May. Weather can change rapidly, especially during the winter and the late-summer thunderstorm season. Sudden heavy rains caused by thunderstorms can drop the temperature 50 degrees in a few minutes.

Snowfall is fairly rare at the lower elevations of the park, and it melts in a few hours. Snow may linger on the highest peaks for a day or two after a storm. Winter at the lower elevations is quite pleasant, and winter storms rarely last

The San Jacinto Mountains form a striking skyline from Eureka Peak.

more than a day or two and are usually followed by several days or even weeks of sunny, mild weather. Spring weather is generally mild and stable, though occasional windstorms may occur. From May through September, daytime temperatures can exceed 100 F, though nights are still cool.

July brings the North American Monsoon, a seasonal invasion of moist, tropical air moving northwest from the Gulf of Mexico. The main effect of the monsoon is to raise humidities from the usual teens or single digits to 50 percent or more, and to trigger afternoon thunderstorms. These thunderstorms lash the mountain peaks and ridges with lightning and often bring short, heavy rains. Plan your outings to be off high peaks and ridges by midday during the monsoon. The sudden runoff from these storms can cause flooding in dry washes and canyons miles from the storm itself, which is why you should never camp or park a vehicle in a dry wash. Rarely, an unusual surge of tropical moisture brings general rain to the region, lasting for several days. More typically, the monsoon follows a surge-and-break pattern, where several days or a week of daily afternoon thunderstorms are followed by several days where few storms form. Even during wetter periods of the monsoon, mornings are usually clear, with the first puffy cumuli appearing by late morning. The monsoon moisture is blocked by the coastal mountains, so Joshua Tree and the southeast California deserts often experience afternoon thunderstorms while the coastal cities remain dry.

The monsoon usually ends by mid-September, resulting in clear, dry, cool weather. Though the lower elevations in the park may still exceed 80 degrees Fahrenheit, the extreme heat of summer is over. Along with spring, fall is the best time to explore the park.

Heat and Dehydration

Summer heat is a serious hazard in the desert elevations. During hot weather it is safer, as well as more enjoyable, to hike early in the day to avoid the afternoon heat. Always take plenty of water, even when the weather isn't scorching hot. The dry desert air, where the humidity often drops below 10 percent, causes insensible moisture loss from your skin and can lead to dehydration. People active in the desert often need a gallon or more of water per day. Sports drinks that replace electrolytes are also useful. Protection both from the heat and the sun is important: A lightweight sun hat is an essential, as are good sunglasses that protect your eyes from damaging infrared and ultraviolet radiation.

Prolonged dehydration and exposure to heat can lead to heat exhaustion, in which the body's heat-regulating mechanism begins to break down. Symptoms include weakness, pale, clammy skin, profuse sweating, and possible unconsciousness. Move the victim to as cool a place as possible, provide shade and electrolyte-replacement drinks, and help the body's cooling efforts by removing excess clothing and providing ventilation.

If untreated, heat exposure can result in sunstroke, a life-threatening medical emergency caused by the failure of the body's heat-regulation system. Sunstroke comes on suddenly and is marked by hot, dry skin as opposed to the pale, clammy skin of heat-exhaustion victims. Additional symptoms include a full, fast pulse, rapid breathing that later becomes shallow and faint, dilated pupils, early loss of consciousness, involuntary muscle twitching, convulsions, and a body temperature of 105 degrees or higher. Treat the victim immediately by moving him or her to a cool location, removing as much clothing as possible, making certain the airway is open, and using wet cloths or water to reduce body temperature. If cold packs are available, they should be placed around the neck, under the arms, and at the ankles, where blood vessels lie close to the skin. Transport the victim to medical care as soon as possible.

Hypothermia

Even in the summer, desert nights are often cool, and in the winter, nights can be downright cold. Winter storms can bring windy, rainy weather and occasionally snow to Joshua Tree National Park. Continuous exposure to chilling weather where your body is steadily losing more heat than it produces can slowly lower your body temperature, resulting in hypothermia. Cool winds, especially with rain, are the most dangerous because the heat loss is insidious.

Hypothermia is a life-threatening condition. Its initial symptoms are subtle and can easily be missed by the inexperienced, but that is the stage where field treatment is the most effective. Episodes of shivering are the first sign that the body is losing heat—the shivering mechanism increases production of heat by muscle action. Although breathing and pulse usually remain normal during this stage, grogginess and muddled thinking are often present, which makes it difficult to recognize hypothermia in yourself. If a member of the party seems confused about where they are or the goal for the outing, be on the alert.

As hypothermia becomes worse, shivering becomes violent. This is the first sign that the body is losing control of its heat-producing mechanism. A marked inability to think and a short attention span, along with slow, shallow breathing and a slow, weak pulse, are serious warning signs. At this stage, you have a medical emergency and the victim must be rewarmed with external heat, as his body is no longer capable of producing enough heat to warm itself. The best source of heat is other people. Ideally, someone should share a sleeping bag with the victim. Hot-water bottles wrapped in clothing can be used, but care must be taken not to burn the victim, who can't sense that objects against his skin are too hot. Hot drinks can help, but only if the victim is fully conscious.

Severe hypothermia is present when shivering stops, followed by unconsciousness, little or no breathing, and a weak, irregular, or nonexistent pulse. The victim's only hope of survival is immediate transport to a medical facility.

Clearly, prevention is the best treatment for hypothermia. It can be completely avoided by wearing enough warm and protective clothing to avoid chilling and by eating and drinking regularly so that your body continues to produce heat. During the winter or in the high country, be prepared for weather changes with several layers of clothing, including wicking underwear, synthetic pants and shirts, a pile or fleece jacket, and a wind- and waterproof outer-shell layer. Synthetic fibers such as polyester don't absorb water when wet and retain most of their insulting ability. In wet weather avoid cotton, which absorbs water like a sponge and dries very slowly. Rescue teams in the Pacific Northwest have a saying: "Cotton Kills."

Water Purification

On day outings you should carry all the water you'll need. Because surface water is rare in Joshua Tree, backpackers should also plan to carry all the water they will need. If you do find surface water, always purify or filter it before use. Purifiers, which include halide chemicals, some filter-based devices, and ultraviolet-light units, remove viruses as well as bacteria and cysts. Most filters do not remove viruses, but luckily virus-borne diseases are uncommon in this area. Filters improve the taste of the water, but are slow, heavy, and bulky compared to chemical purifiers. Keep filters clean by replacing the filter element or cleaning it as per the manufacturer's instructions. Murky desert water has a way of clogging filters quickly, so use a prefilter if one is available for your unit.

When using halide purifying agents, follow the instructions carefully, especially in regard to the wait time for the chemical to complete its work. Never add flavored drink mixes to water until the wait time has lapsed, because the ascorbic acid (vitamin C) used in many drink mixes neutralizes the purifying agent.

Bringing water to a boil purifies it at any altitude, but this uses a lot of fuel and leaves you with a hot, flat-tasting drink. Pouring boiled water back and forth between two pots cools it off and restores the dissolved air that makes water taste better.

Old Mines

Old mines and prospects are common in this desert park. While hazardous areas ideally are signed and fenced, in practice this doesn't always happen, and every year some people ignore the warnings and get hurt or killed. Expect to find open mine shafts in any area with signs of mining activity, such as the ruins of structures or heaps of tailings—waste rock dumped from mines. Vertical shafts are an especially serious hazard, because even shallow pits can cause a serious or fatal fall. Be especially cautious in brushy areas. Use a flashlight when walking at night off-trail, even around camp. Never approach the edge of a pit or shaft: The edges are often unstable or undercut and there's no way to tell

Cholla-cactus spines are sharp and invisibly barbed.

how deep they are. Stay out of all mine shafts. They are often unstable, there can be partially covered or hidden vertical shafts, and poisonous or radioactive gasses may be present.

Cacti and Other Plant Hazards

The Mojave Desert, which covers the western half of the park, has relatively few species of cactus, while the lower and warmer Sonoran Desert in the eastern half has more. All cacti have spines. The spines on large cacti such as barrel cacti are easy to see and avoid, but some are more subtle. Hedgehog cacti tend to blend in with clumps of grass on rock ledges, and scramblers and rock climbers should watch where they place their hands. Most species of cholla cactus propagate by means of joints—the outer segments of branches easily break off and cling to animals or humans that brush against them. Cholla cactus spines are fine, sharp, and microscopically barbed. You'll need a comb or a pair of sticks to dislodge the joints. Deeply embedded cholla spines, caused by falling on a cactus, may need pliers for removal. Dogs are especially adept at getting cholla spines deeply embedded in their mouths, which may require a visit to the vet.

Plenty of other desert plants have developed spines for defense. Some agaves and yuccas have stiff swordlike leaves with sharp points that can do serious damage to the desert explorer unfortunate enough to fall on one. Catclaw is a low bush that often grows in thickets and is covered with curved spines that catch on clothing and skin. All these sharp bits of plant tend to end up on the ground, so check the ground carefully before you sit down or set up a tent. Users of air mattresses and self-inflating foam pads have to be especially careful. Some desert campers have given up on self-inflating pads and use closed-cell foam pads instead, which aren't as comfortable but do have the advantages of being lighter and immune to punctures.

Animal Hazards

Rattlesnakes are present throughout Joshua Tree National Park and are most active from March through October. Many newcomers to desert hiking are scared off by the thought of being attacked by a rattlesnake, but rattlesnakes are not aggressive and go out of their way to avoid an encounter. They usually sense your presence before you are aware of them and move quietly out of the way. If an intruder does get too close or the snake is surprised or cornered, it uses its rattle as a warning well before you come in range of its strike.

The rattling sound, which the snake creates by rapidly shaking the rattle on its tail, is an unmistakable sound but one that can be difficult to locate, especially in grass or brush. When you first hear it, stop and locate the snake visually before moving quietly around it. Snakes sometimes den up together, so watch for other snakes as you avoid the first one. Never handle or tease any snake. Most snakebite victims are snake collectors, people working around rock or woodpiles, and people playing with snakes.

Since rattlesnakes can strike no further than approximately half their body length, avoid placing your hands and feet in areas that you cannot see, and walk several feet away from rock overhangs and shady ledges. Bites usually occur on the feet or ankles, so ankle-high hiking boots and loose-fitting long pants will prevent most injuries. Snakes prefer surfaces of about 80 degrees F. This means they like the shade of bushes or rock overhangs in hot weather, and in cool weather they prefer open, sunny ground. Don't confuse commonly found but nonpoisonous bull snakes with rattlesnakes—bull snakes don't have rattles on their tails.

Although rattlesnake bites are not life threatening except in rare cases, usually involving the very young or infirm, the venom can do serious damage to tissue. Since the snake's venom is designed to immobilize mice and other small mammals that are the rattlesnake's usual prey, rattlesnakes usually save their venom for hunting strikes. Warning bites often inject little or no venom. Actually, the main hazards from most accidental rattlesnake bites are panic on the part of the victim and infection caused by the deep puncture wounds. If someone does get bit, keep the victim calm and transport him to medical care as soon as possible. If possible, identify the snake but not at the risk of further bites. Rattlesnake bites can be identified by the two puncture marks from the venom-injecting fangs, in addition to teeth marks. Nonvenomous snakes can certainly bite you but do not leave fang marks.

Mountain lions (also known as pumas or cougars) roam the wilder sections of the park and are occasionally sighted. More often you'll just see their tracks. There have been a few lion attacks on mountain bikers and runners in other parts of California, where the big cats have apparently reacted to fast-moving humans as prey. Lions attack deer, their normal prey, by ambush and will not attack if at a disadvantage or outnumbered. That means that groups are safer than solo hikers. It also means you should make yourself appear as large as possible if you encounter a lion, by standing up straight, spreading your jacket wide, and the like. Experts advise that you avoid eye contact and move away slowly. If attacked, fight back with anything at hand. Many lion encounters involve roaming dogs, so keep dogs on a leash. Remember, dogs are allowed only on roads in the national park, not on the trails.

Skunks, mice, and other rodents are nocturnal animals that often become camp robbers, especially at heavily used campsites. All of them are persistent and can easily ruin your night's sleep. A rodent-proof campsite box or portable rodent-proof container solves the problem. Food left in a vehicle is not safe from mice. When backpacking, hang your food if possible, and leave all pack pockets open so rodents can explore the enticing residual smells without having to chew their way in.

Winter and spring rains can sometimes bring out a few mosquitoes in the desert but rarely in large numbers. Because mosquitoes can transmit West Nile virus, use repellent and sleep in a tent when they are present. Gnats can sometimes occur in large numbers, especially after a wet winter. Deet in various concentrations seems to be the most effective repellent against both mosquitoes and gnats.

Scorpions are common in the park but are not dangerous, except to individuals who are allergic to their venom. Scorpion stings can be avoided by always watching where you place your hands and feet. Kick rocks and logs before picking them up, keep clothing and bedding packed or in a tent or vehicle when not in use, and always shake out clothing and footwear before putting them on.

Africanized bees, originally released in South America, have spread north through Mexico into the Sonoran and Mojave Deserts. These bees look identical to the common European honeybee but are more aggressive. Since they interbreed freely, even domestic hives can be Africanized. Avoid all concentrations of bees, especially hives and swarms. If attacked, drop your pack and run. Protect your eyes and don't swat at the bees. The smell of crushed bees incites Africanized bees to attack more aggressively. Africanized bees won't pursue for more than a half mile, and in fact, most victims are old, infirm, or otherwise unable to escape. If shelter such as a building or vehicle is available, use it. Otherwise, try to get into brush or dense foliage, which confuses the bees.

Black-widow spiders, identifiable by the red hourglass-shaped mark on the underside, have a neurotoxic venom and can inflict a dangerous bite. At first the bite is not especially painful, but symptoms, which can include difficulty breathing, develop rapidly, and victims should get medical care immediately. There is no specific field treatment; young children should be transported to a hospital as soon as possible.

The brown recluse spider inflicts a bite that is slow to heal and sometimes causes extensive tissue damage at the site but is not generally life threatening. Both types of spiders are more common around man-made structures such as woodpiles than they are in the wild. They like dark, hidden areas, so be especially careful picking up downed wood or rocks.

The dangerous-looking centipede can inflict a painful bite and also irritate skin with its sharp, clawed feet, but it is not life threatening.

Kissing bugs, also known as cone-nose bugs or assassin bugs, are obnoxious insects that live in rodent nests and feed on mammal blood at night. The bite is painless and the victim is often unaware of the bite for several days, until a large, itchy welt develops. Kissing-bug bites usually heal in a week or so. Kissing bugs are not a problem during the cooler months, but during the warmer half of the year, they give desert campers one more reason to sleep in a fully closed net tent.

Ticks occur rarely in the desert. If ticks are discovered, though, do a careful full body search every day. It's important to remove embedded ticks before they have a chance to transmit disease, which takes a day or more. Some ticks carry Lyme disease, which can cause serious complications if not treated.

People who have a known allergic reaction to specific insect stings are at special risk. Since this reaction can develop rapidly and be life threatening, such people should check with their doctors to see if desensitization treatment is recommended. They should also carry insect-sting kits prescribed by their doctors.

Wildfires

Portions of Joshua Tree National Park have been burned by recent wildfires. Though at first glance the desert would seem to be fireproof, wet winters can trigger the growth of seasonal vegetation such as flowering plants and grasses, which dry out in the summer heat and create a fire hazard. Also, the introduction of exotic grasses has increased the amount of ground cover available to carry fire between formerly isolated bushes and other plants.

History

Natives

Prehistoric people apparently discovered the Pinto Basin area in the eastern portion of what is now Joshua Tree National Park as early as 9,300 years ago. Although to the modern eye the desert appears barren, the natives found plenty of food and other resources. Cactus fruit, acorns, berries, mesquite pods, piñon nuts, and various seeds were available. They also hunted deer, bighorn sheep, birds, reptiles, and rabbits. Plant and animal materials were used to make cordage, thread, baskets, mats, seed beaters, clothing, and many other tools and implements.

By the time the first European explorers reached the area in the 1850s, the Joshua Tree area was occupied by the Serrano, Chemehuevi (also known as the Southern Paiutes), and Cahuilla peoples. Apparently there were no fixed boundaries between these three groups, as they moved around the desert as resources and populations fluctuated. The Cahuilla and Serrano natives primarily lived in small villages near reliable water sources such as the Oasis of Mara near the present park headquarters. They exploited the resources of the western and southern portions of the park. The Chemehuevi appear to have occupied the eastern portions of the park, living in temporary hunting and gathering camps during the spring and summer and gathering in large villages during the cold winter months.

Explorers

Although California's coast was explored and settled by the Spanish in the sixteenth century, these Europeans came by ship and showed little interest in the forbiddingly dry desert to the east of the coastal mountains. Probably the first white man to pass through the Joshua Tree country was mountain man Pauline Weaver, who in 1842, while the area was still part of Mexico, pioneered a route across the Morongo Valley, past the Oasis of Mara, and eastward. His road was occasionally used by the few hardy travelers willing to brave the desert.

Barker Lake, in the Wonderland of Rocks, is the largest of the old rancher's stock watering ponds found in the park.

The first official mention of the Joshua Tree area was the report of an 1855 government survey, which described the Oasis of Mara and an old road leading east through the desert. At first the Oasis of Mara was called Palm Springs, but in the 1870s the name was changed to Twentynine Palms.

Miners and Ranchers

After the famous California gold rush to the Sierra Nevada began to play out in the 1860s, prospectors began to look for other rich areas. Deserts have always attracted prospectors and miners because the lack of soil and vegetation exposes rocks and minerals to easy view. Prospectors used the Oasis of Mara as a base camp while exploring the rugged mountains to the south. In 1865 the first mining claim was filed for the Jeff Davis Mine in Rattlesnake Canyon in the northwest corner of the future park. Although most prospects never had enough valuable minerals to be developed into productive mines, there was always hope, and prospectors looked into every corner of the Joshua Tree country hoping to strike it rich. There were also plenty of swindlers, bilking investors by making false claims or even seeding a prospect with rich ore brought in from somewhere else. "Quartz" Wilson was one such prospector, who often exasperated his partners with exaggerated claims. Still, Wilson and partner Tom Lyon managed to set off a minor boom in the Dale Mining District when they discovered the Virginia Dale Mine in the 1880s. Later, Wilson found a rich vein of gold at what would become the Eldorado Mine.

Serious, productive mines like the Eldorado required food, timber, machinery, and other supplies which had to be hauled across the desert from distant towns such as Amboy and San Bernadino. Teamsters used horses and mules to haul heavy loads of freight in wagons across the desert, and they established roads across the desert, using springs such as the Oasis of Mara as watering and resting places. Many of the modern roads in the Joshua Tree area follow the routes of the old freight roads.

Ranchers were attracted to the desert as winter range for their cattle, which spent the summer months in lusher mountain pastures to the west. One such early rancher was Bill McHaney, who came to the Oasis of Mara in 1879 and used it as a base camp for both cattle ranching and prospecting. The largest cattle outfit was Barker and Shay, who ran cattle throughout the western portion of Joshua Tree and developed numerous water sources, such as Barker Dam, White Tank, Squaw Tank, Live Oak Tank, and Ivanpah Tank.

Another famous resident was William F. Keys, who came to the area in 1910 and soon established a home. He raised a family and worked at mines and mills as well as ranching, living at the Desert Queen Ranch until his death in 1969. Tours of the ranch are led by park rangers. Although the ranch buildings have deteriorated since Keys died, there are now efforts to restore the ranch site.

Wells and windmills such as this one were another source of water for the early ranchers.

The town of Twentynine Palms was established near the Oasis of Mara in the early twentieth century as people began to come to the clear, dry air of the desert as a cure for respiratory problems aggravated by the pollution of big cities. Most of the original settlers camped at the Oasis of Mara before choosing a site, digging a well, and building a house. Automobiles made desert travel much easier, and increasing numbers of people came from the coastal cities both to live and to see the area. Human impacts increased rapidly as people dug more and more wells and the resulting use lowered the water table. The Oasis of Mara, so crucial to both the natives and the historical use of the area, dried up in 1942. Many desert visitors dug up cactus and other desert plants to use as ornamentals at their homes in the coast cities, and

A small granite tablet marks the site where Bill Keys shot Worth Bagley over a road dispute.

there was plenty of thoughtless vandalism of the "worthless" desert, such as the burning of Joshua trees.

One person who was dismayed by the destruction of the desert was Minerva Hoyt. In the late 1920s she led an effort to protect the area, and in 1936 President Franklin Roosevelt signed a proclamation creating the original 825,000-acre Joshua Tree National Monument.

National Monument to National Park

Not everyone was happy with the new national monument. Although existing mining claims and private property within the monument were not affected by the designation, mining interests in particular tried to get the federal government to rescind the monument. In 1950 their efforts were partially successful: The Old Dale Mining District was removed from the monument, reducing the monument's size to 560,000 acres. Today the numerous roads, abandoned prospects, mines, and mining equipment littering the Old Dale area reminds us of what might have happened had the entire monument been rescinded.

During the second half of the twentieth century, as the population of California and the western United States grew rapidly, so did outdoor recreation and an awareness that special places such as Joshu Tree and the California deserts should be preserved. In 1994 Congress created Joshua Tree National Park and expanded it to 790,000 acres—nearly the size of the original monument. Most of the additions were on the east and south sides, including the Coxcomb and Eagle Mountains. Most of the new area is also designated wilderness, which gives the backcountry hiker a large, seldom-visited region of the park to explore.

Natural History

Why a Desert?

Deserts form for several reasons, but there are two main factors that maintain the desert climate at Joshua Tree. The first is a strong high pressure region that forms in the eastern Pacific during much of the year. From spring through fall this persistent high diverts low-pressure systems with their associated stormy weather to the north, keeping California in a dry weather pattern. The other factor is the rain shadow effect. During the winter, when the high breaks down and moisture-laden storms move in from the Pacific Ocean, they must cross the coastal mountains before reaching the Joshua Tree area. As the moist air reaches the steep terrain, it is forced to rise, which cools the air and causes it to drop most of its moisture on the mountains in the form of snow and rain. Descending the eastern, lee sides of the mountains, the air warms rapidly and there is little moisture left to form clouds and rain.

As mentioned earlier, there is a second rainy period in late summer when the North American Monsoon brings moisture northwest across New Mexico and Arizona from the Gulf of Mexico. Because Joshua Tree is so far from the source of this moisture, the monsoon is weaker here than it is in areas further to the southeast, such as northern Mexico.

Geography and Geology

Joshua Tree National Park is located at the eastern end of Southern California's Transverse Mountain Range. Most North American mountain ranges trend generally north and south, but the ranges that are encompassed by Joshua Tree National Park run east to west, as do the ranges to the west, the San Bernadino and San Jacinto Mountains. Elevations range from less than 1,000 feet above sea level at the southeast corner of the park to 5,813 feet at Quail Mountain. In general, the eastern half of the park is lower, lying between 1,000 and 3,000 feet, while the western half is higher, lying between 3,000 and 5,000 feet.

The Little San Bernadino and Hexie Mountains dominate the western portion of the park, while the Cottonwood and Eagle Mountains lie along the southern border. A large valley, the Pinto Basin, separates the southern ranges from the Pinto Mountains, which are along the northern border of the park. The Coxcomb Mountains are the easternmost range in the park.

Joshua Tree National Park is noted for its striking landscape of granite boulders set among unusual desert plants. Many of the rocks exposed in the park are metamorphic rocks, meaning that they have been changed from their original state. Rock is formed by either volcanic action, such as lava flows, ash falls, or cinder deposits, by deposition of sediments such as mud or sand, or by precipitation of particles from water. When these volcanic or sedimentary rocks are buried deep in the earth by additional layers of rock, extreme temperatures and pressures change the rock into new forms: metamorphic rocks.

The metamorphic rocks in Joshua Tree are the result of at least two large-scale mountain-building events. It is now accepted among geologists that the continents are huge plates of lighter rock floating on the denser, partially molten rocks of the Earth's mantle. Slow but immense currents within the mantle move the continental plates around, so that they occasionally collide to form supercontinents, then separate to become the smaller continents that we have at present.

Around 1,700 million years ago, the Joshua Tree area was part of a supercontinent we call Rodinia, which consisted of present-day Scandinavia, Greenland, North America, Australia, and Antarctica, all jammed together. An immense mountain range called the Transrodinian Mountains stretched across the entire supercontinent. This is why some of the oldest rocks in Joshua Tree, granitic rocks known as gneiss (pronounced *nice*), are also found near the South Pole and in Australia and northern Europe. These metamorphic rocks date back two billion years, before any life formed on the planet.

About 800 million years ago, Rodinia drifted apart, but by 280 million years ago, North America was part of another supercontinent, Pangaea. The breakup of Pangaea, around 200 million years ago, caused another round of mountain building as the western edge of the North American continental plate collided with the Pacific plate to the west. This period was when the ancestors to the present-day Sierra Nevada and Rocky Mountains were created.

When continental plates collide, they can either slip alongside each other or collide directly. The westward movement of the North American plate during the breakup of Pangaea ushered in a long period of collision with the Pacific plate. Since ocean plates are thinner and heavier than continental plates, the Pacific plate slid under the North American plate in a process called subduction. This lifts the edge of the continental plate into mountain ranges. The diving ocean plate melts as it plunges into the Earth's mantle, causing pockets of liquid rock (called magma) to rise toware the surface. If the magma actually reaches the surface, it forms volcanoes as the liquid rock, released from the

Dikes are formed when molten rock forces its way into weaknesses in the bedrock. They are often highly mineralized.

tremendous pressures found deep in the Earth, explodes into the air or pours forth as lava. Other bodies of magma cool and solidify before reaching the surface, forming intruded masses of rock called plutons.

After a long period of subduction, large-scale mountain building, and vulcanism, the direction of collision between the Pacific and North American plates changed to more of a sliding motion, starting about thirty million years ago. The Pacific plate is moving northwest, and the North American plate is moving southeast, meeting along the San Andreas Fault. This zone of collision runs from the Gulf of California, past Joshua Tree National Park, through San Francisco Bay, and up to Cape Mendocino. From Keys View in the park, you can clearly trace the line of the San Andreas Fault along a line of low hills in the Coachella Valley below. Uplifting caused by motion along the San Andreas fault system eventually created the Transverse Range, including the mountains of Joshua Tree.

As the ancient roots of two mountain ranges were being uplifted into the present Transverse Range by plate collision and faulting, other forces were just as avidly tearing the mountains down. Water is the prime agent of erosion. Falling in the form of rain or snow and running off, water erodes the mountains by both dissolving the rocks and by physically carrying away particles ranging in size from silt to sand to pebbles and even boulders. The eroded material is either carried to the sea, if the climate is wet enough and the rivers large enough, or is deposited in basins at the foot of the mountains during drier periods. Joshua Tree has gone through repeated periods of cooler, wetter climate followed by warmer, arid periods such as the present, as ice ages have come and gone during the last 1.6 million years. Although no glaciers formed in the Joshua Tree area, the wetter climate of the ice ages allowed deep soil and lush vegetation to form, and the increased precipitation caused erosion of the mountains to accelerate. During warmer, arid periods, erosion still occurs but at a slower rate.

Some of the valleys in the park, such as Pinto Basin, are the result of erosion that carried material away to lower country. Others, such as Pleasant Valley, are the result of downward movement along fault lines.

Faults usually create zones of shattered, weakened rock as the rocks move past each other. Canyons often form along faults as water runoff takes advantage of the weakened, more easily erode rock. The Blue Cut is an example of a canyon carved along a fault.

Faults are often responsible for another distinctive desert feature, springs and oases. Groundwater is often blocked or diverted by a fault and makes its way to the surface. An example is the Oasis of Mara near the Oasis Visitor Center in Twentynine Palms, where the fault scarp is plainly visible from the nature trail.

As the granite, gneiss, and other metamorphic rocks that have long been buried deep in the Earth under great pressure are gradually exposed, the release of pressure causes cracks to form. Such cracks, which have no movement along them, are called joints, in contrast to faults, where the rock on one side moves relative to the other. Especially during wet periods, groundwater soaks downward along the joints, dissolving the rock while it is still buried under the top layers of soil. By the time the rocks are exposed at the surface, they have eroded into the rounded piles of boulders that are such a distinctive feature of Joshua Tree.

Erosion continues to work on the exposed rocks through two processes of weathering. Physical weathering causes the physical destruction of rock by the levering action of growing plant roots and the freezing of water. Both exert a tremendous force on the sides of cracks, splitting large and small pieces from the rocks, where gravity carries them downward. Chemical weathering is the dissolving of rocks by rainwater, snowmelt, and groundwater. Weathered-rock grains gather at the foot of boulders and cliffs to form the basis for soil, which is enriched by the decay of organic material and the actions of microorganisms.

The processes of erosion in dry climates produces the unique landforms found in desert areas such as Joshua Tree. Broad desert valleys, which may or may not have outlets to lower valleys and eventually to the sea, abruptly transition to steep-sided mountain ranges. Alluvial fans spread out from the bases of the mountains, formed by debris brought down the steep canyons by flash floods. Where several alluvial fans overlap, they form bajadas, broad overlapping aprons of sand, gravel, and rocks skirting the base of the mountain ranges. Inselburgs, isolated steep-sided rock hills, rise from the bajada slopes. Arroyos and washes, dry most of the time, emerge from the mountain canyons and drain the valleys. Washes that flow into basins that have no outlet create playas, flat plains of lake-bed sediments formed on the rare occasions when water flows down the washes to the valley floor. During the ice ages many playas became lakes, fed by the increased runoff. When the climate dried out, so did the lakes. Windblown sand from the dry lake beds sometimes accumulates to form sand dunes, such as those in Pinto Basin. Desert pavements consist of a surface layer of many small rocks and pebbles, lying close together and protecting the sandy soil underneath from erosion.

Two Deserts Meet

Joshua Tree National Park is nearly equally divided between the high Mojave Desert (*Mojave* may be spelled with either a *j* or an *h*, but as a Spanish word it is always pronounced *Mo-haa-vee*) in the western portion of the park and the low Sonoran desert in the lower eastern area. The Sonoran Desert is broken into subdivsions, and the westernmost portion, surrounding the Colorado River and extending to Joshua Tree, is often known as the Colorado Desert.

Each desert has its own ecology of plants and animals, but there is a transition zone where plants from either desert mingle with the other.

Sonoran (1,000 to 3,000 feet)

The hotter Sonoran desert in the park is characterized by creosote bushes, which cover vast areas but maintain a dignified distance from each other due to the scarcity of water. Actually, creosote bushes excrete a chemical inhibitor from their roots, which prevents competing creosote bushes from sprouting too close. Ocotillo, spindly plants about 8 to 10 feet tall that have several long, narrow stems sprouting from a common base, and the cuddly looking teddybear cholla (also called Bigelow cholla) are other distinctive plants of the Sonoran.

Mojave (3,000 to 5,000 feet)

Somewhat cooler and wetter than the Sonoran, the Mojave Desert is the home of the park's namesake plant, the Joshua tree. Not a tree at all but a type of yucca, Joshua trees have a single trunk but branch out seemingly at random above, creating a weird, scraggly silhouette. Joshua trees growing in favorable areas reach 30 feet or more in height.

Desert Adaptations

Just how do plants and animals manage to survive in an environment with just a few inches of rain per year and summer temperatures that often exceed 110 degrees F? The answer lies in a remarkable series of adaptations made by the processes of evolution.

Plants

Plants of the Sonoran and Mojave Deserts have adopted a variety of different and sometimes surprising methods to survive and even thrive in arid conditions. Water is indeed the stuff of life; most plants are 80 to 90 percent water and depend on it for the chemical processes, such as photosynthesis, that create food and sustain life, as well for structural support, by maintaining the shape and strength of cells, and for cooling by evaporation from the leaves.

One group of desert plants cheats a bit by growing near sources of water, usually along canyon bottoms where groundwater is near the surface or at rare springs and oases. Plants such as Fremont cottonwood and various willows, which require large amounts of groundwater, take advantage of the situation and grow in ribbons along the streambeds and in clumps around springs. These riparian life zones are a special case of nondesert life finding a small niche in otherwise arid country.

Another group of plants avoids meeting the desert head on by remaining in the ground as seeds until conditions are favorable. These plants, technically annuals but better termed ephemerals, can wait as seeds for years until enough moisture comes in the form of winter or summer rains. When the conditions are met, the plants quickly germinate and often appear within a few days. Because the extra moisture is short-lived, ephemerals typically complete their entire life cycle in just a few weeks. These plants produce the glorious flower shows that occur some years and carpet the desert with millions of flowers, delighting the astonished visitor.

All is not as simple as it seems, because extra moisture alone doesn't trigger the germination of the ephemerals. Not only does a minimum amount of moisture have to fall, it has to fall in the right way. Gentle, prolonged rains are much more likely to trigger germination than torrential downpours. Temperature is also important. Plants that germinate during the winter need cool days and nights, but plants that grow following the summer rains need warm days and nights. So the lower-elevation Sonoran Desert plains and foothills in the eastern portion of the park tend to produce flower shows during late winter, while at the higher elevations of the Mojave Desert in the western sections of the park, flowers tend to appear during early spring. The onset of summer heat marks the end of the flowers, as they quickly wilt.

The plants that most people think of as desert plants are the perennials, which face the desert through an entire year of extremes and may have to endure successive drier-than-normal years.
Even desert plants have their limits, but most have a remarkable ability to endure long droughts. The extreme drought in the Southwest between 1995 and 2004 has shown just how tough the desert plants are. So far they have not died off in massive numbers like the piñon pines and juniper trees have at higher elevations.

Plants adapt to year-round life in the desert by either being drought tolerators or drought avoiders. The drought avoiders manage to avoid drought stress by either adopting extreme measures to conserve water—the water savers—or by being more efficient at collecting water—the water spenders. The savers conserve

Blue Canterbury bells like to tuck in close to granite boulders.

water through various methods. Some limit transpiration of moisture through their leaves by only allowing it to take place for short periods each day. Others have a waxy coating that slows the loss of moisture. Still others reduce the surface area that they expose to the drying air. Some plants move or curl their leaves to avoid exposure to the sun during the hottest time of day, while others drop their leaves entirely during dry periods. Some plants can even partially die, dropping entire branches to conserve life in the remaining portions of the plant.

Water savers typically have extensive root systems, much larger than you would expect from the size of the aboveground plant. Some plants, especially cactus, even grow special rain roots within a few hours after rainfall, increasing the plant's ability to quickly take in moisture from the soil before it disappears.

Cacti are among the best examples of water savers, capable of storing large amounts of water within their interior pulpy flesh. Barrel cacti are prime examples. While the interior of these plants are filled with soft pulp, their support comes from woody ribs that circle the plant below the skin. As the pulp absorbs water and expands, the ribs move further apart. You can see this effect clearly from the outside. Barrel cacti in dry conditions have accordion pleats that are very close together, while plants that have received a moisture bonanza have pleats that are much further apart, almost giving the plant a bloated appearance.

Cacti have other remarkable adaptations. Normally, green plants produce food by taking in carbon dioxide during the day and creating complex carbohydrates through photosynthesis with sunlight. But this means opening the plant's surface pores, which means that moisture escapes. Some cactus only open their pores during the night, when the humidity is higher and temperatures lower. They store the carbon dioxide as organic acids and then process it into carbohydrates during the day while the pores are closed.

Because water-saving plants spend water, and therefore energy, at a low rate, they are generally slow-growing, long-lived plants. A barrel cactus may only grow a couple of inches during the first eight years of its life.

Water spenders take the opposite approach. These desert-adapted plants have the ability to extract more water from the soil than nondesert plants, so they can continue transpiration from their leaves even during the heat of the day. Like some of the water savers, many water spenders have large root systems. Some, like the palo verde and mesquite trees, reach far down to the water table. Another adaptation is the ability, even under dry conditions, to send new roots into moist areas. Even more remarkable is the fact that many water spenders can become water savers under prolonged drought, slowing down growth and waiting. Then, when wet weather finally does arrive, they grow at much faster rates than nondesert plants.

Drought-tolerating plants have the ability to survive much more moisture loss than comparable nondesert plants. Most shade plants start to wilt after only a 1 or 2 percent water loss, but drought-tolerant desert plants can withstand 30 to 40 percent losses. Most of the adaptations that allow plants to endure drought are at the cell level.

The creosote bush, most common in the Sonoran Desert but also found in the Mojave Desert, is a fine example of a drought-tolerating plant. During extended dry periods the creosote bush sheds its mature leaves, as well as twigs and branches, but retains its small, young leaves. These leaves can lose 70 percent of their moisture and still be actively producing food for the plant. When moisture comes, the presence of the small leaves allow creosote bushes to take immediate advantage. Creosote is so drought-tolerant that it grows in desert areas where it may not rain for a year or more and the summer high temperatures often exceed 120 degrees.

Animals

Desert animals have a major advantage over plants: They can move to more favorable locations when necessary, whereas plants have to endure whatever conditions occur at the place where they took root. Animals can take advantage of microclimates—changes in temperature and moisture over distances of a few feet—to find more suitable habitat. The shady area under a bush may be dozens of degrees cooler than a patch of bare ground a few feet away. And the climate under a rock may be many times more humid than the top of that same rock.

Desert air temperatures, measured at the official 5 feet above the ground, can vary from a high of 110 to a low of 60 degrees during a summer day and night. At the surface, daytime temperatures can reach 155 degrees, while at night, because the ground loses heat by radiation to the sky, temperatures can drop to 40 degrees. Ground-dwelling animals such as snakes, insects, and rodents have to find some way to endure such extremes. The answer lies beneath the surface. Because of the insulating properties of desert soil, the temperature a couple of feet down only varies about 30 degrees, and at about 4 feet, there is no temperature change at all. By living at least part of the time in burrows, desert animals escape the temperature extremes and also have a more humid environment.

Some animals don't survive drought as individuals. Like ephemeral plants, they take advantage of wet periods to reproduce. For example, tadpole shrimp eggs can survive for years in the baked dry mud left after temporary rain pools evaporate. When the rains come, the eggs hatch, and the tadpole shrimp emerges to complete its life cycle before the pool dries up.

Many reptiles, such as snakes and lizards, are well adapted for desert life. Because they are cold-blooded, the body temperature of reptiles stays close to that of their environment. It's commonly believed that reptiles revel in the fierce desert heat, but in reality they would quickly die if left exposed to summer ground temperatures. Rattlesnakes, for example, function best at body temperatures around 85 degrees, so they seek out places that are comfortable, such as shade on hot days and sunny rock slabs on cool ones. In extreme heat, rattlesnakes retreat into burrows abandoned by other animals, where their low metabolism rates allow them to endure many days between meals. During prolonged cold temperatures, rattlesnakes and other reptiles become dormant, remaining in this state sometimes for months.

Although many desert reptiles will drink water when they have a chance, as a rule they get most or all of their water from their prey. In the case of rattlesnakes and other desert snakes, the mice and other small rodents that they eat provide most of their water. Desert tortoises, unlike most desert reptiles, are vegetarian, and they are capable of getting nearly all the water they need from grass and other low vegetation. Desert tortoises are active for about half the year, escaping the heat of midday in burrows that they dig. The winter half of the year is spent dormant in burrows.

The fringe-toed lizard has projecting scales on its hind feet that it uses to run across the areas of fine, windblown sand that it inhabits. This lizard often ends its run over the sand with a dive, burrowing rapidly into the cooler sand and continuing to swim under the surface for some distance. The fringe-toed lizard has overlapping eyelids and ear flaps to keep sand out, and special sand-trapping nasal passages to allow it to breathe under the sand without getting sand in its lungs. The ability to swim under the sand not only keeps the lizard cool but also hides it from predators.

The sidewinder rattlesnake has a unique method of moving on loose sand. As the name implies, this small rattlesnake (about 18 to 32 inches in length) moves forward by throwing its body sideways in a series of loops. It appears to be crawling sideways in a flowing curve. The tracks left are unmistakable: a series of parallel lines at an angle to the sidewinder's direction of travel. Not only is sidewinding an efficient method of movement in the sandy areas that sidewinders prefer, it also reduces the area of the snake's body in contact with the sand, helping to keep its temperature down.

Spadefoot toads carry dormancy to an extreme. Adult spadefoots spend most of the year dormant underground, waiting for the summer rains. Within an hour of the first heavy rain, the toads emerge into the temporary pools, calling to each other in loud bleats. After mating, the eggs are deposited in the temporary ponds, where they hatch in less than seventy-two hours. The hatchlings go through the larval stage in as little as ten days, and the adult spadefoot toads appear in time to burrow into the beds of the drying ponds. The name *spadefoot* comes from the sharp-edged projection on the rear of their hind legs, which they use to help dig backward into the mud as they bury themselves. If the summer rains fail, the spadefoot can survive another year.

Larger mammals and most birds can't use burrows to escape the heat. Birds, of course, have the advantage of wings. They can fly to cooler resting sites in trees or fly high above the ground where the air is cooler. One of the desert's enduring sights is that of the vulture or raven circling in updrafts thousands of feet above the ground, waiting patiently for some hapless rodent or reptile to lose the fight to survive. Flight also lets birds find springs or water holes at a distance, and some birds leave the desert entirely during the summer, migrating north to cooler climates.

Mourning doves, whose plaintive call is one of the desert's distinctive sounds, live in the desert year round. They can withstand an amazing 30 percent dehydration and can also drink much saltier water than most birds.

Large mammals, though not as common as in wet regions, do survive and even thrive in the desert. Like birds, their mobility gives them an advantage over small mammals and reptiles in finding water. Desert bighorn sheep, which live in some of the most barren portions of the Sonoran and Mojave Deserts, are well adapted to desert life. Although the bighorns do need occasional access to open water, they do get a large amount of moisture from the vegetation they eat. Bighorn sheep prefer rocky mountainsides, where they congregate in small bands high above the canyon floors.

Jackrabbits have huge, heavily veined, thinly furred ears that not only serve the usual rabbit purpose of listening intently for predators but also work as efficient radiators to help the animal lose body heat. Jackrabbits often come out in large numbers after sunset and can be seen jumping in front of cars on desert back roads, where they zigzag in confusion before dashing to safety in the roadside brush.

Kangaroo rats, which as the name implies get around by hopping on their strong hind legs, can survive without any liquid water. Although many other desert animals can go long periods without a drink, most are dependent on water they extract from their prey or from succulent plants. The kangaroo rat actually metabolizes water from dry plant food and can survive completely without water.

The casual visitor to the desert looks at the stark, flat light of the hot midday sun and thinks that the desert is nearly lifeless. In reality, there is much going on beneath the surface, hidden from view. If the visitor spends some time in the desert, he or she soon learns that the desert comes alive at night, after rains, or in cool spells, when desert life ventures forth.

Getting to the Park

Joshua Tree National Park is located about 140 miles east of Los Angeles, between Interstate 10 on the south and Highway 62 on the north. In addition, Highway 177 skirts the eastern border. Nearby cities and towns include Palm Springs and Indio along I–10, and Yucca Valley and Twentynine Palms along Highway 62.

Several airlines serve Palm Springs, southwest of the park. Because there is no public transportation to or around the park, you'll need a car to explore Joshua Tree. There are three main entrances to the park. The West Entrance on Park Boulevard is reached from the town of Joshua Tree off Highway 62. The Oasis Visitor Center and the North Entrance are reached from Highway 62 in Twentynine Palms by turning south on Utah Trail, and the South Entrance is located on the Pinto Basin Road, about 25 miles east of Indio on I-10. There are also two campground and trailhead complexes on dead-end roads along the north side of the park, both reached from Highway 62. Black Rock Canyon Campground and Trailhead and the northwest corner of the park are reached by turning south on Joshua Tree Lane from the town of Yucca Valley, and Indian Cove Campground and Trailhead are reached via Indian Cove Road just west of Twentynine Palms.

Getting around the Park

Two paved roads traverse the park and provide access to most of the campgrounds and trailheads. Park Boulevard connects the West and North Entrances, and the Pinto Basin Road forks off the eastern portion of Park Boulevard at Pinto Wye and traverses Pinto Basin to the Cottonwood Visitor Center and the South Entrance. A number of paved and graded dirt side roads lead to other trailheads, campgrounds, and points of interest. Finally, several primitive, unmaintained dirt roads passable only to four-wheel-drive vehicles lead through some of the remote sections of the park. Most of the park not traversed by roads is designated as wilderness, where the only travel is by non-mechanical means—horses or on foot.

Visitor Centers and Amenities

There are two visitor centers: Oasis Visitor Center at park headquarters on Utah Trail in Twentynine Palms and Cottonwood Visitor Center at the South Entrance on the Pinto Basin Road. Both visitor centers have exhibits and programs explaining the park, as well as bookstores. Park rangers are available to answer questions. Both visitor centers are open daily from 8:00 A.M. to 4:00 P.M.

Campgrounds and Picnic Areas

There are nine campgrounds within the park, all with fireplaces, tables, and toilets. Most charge a daily fee. Campers must bring their own wood from outside the park as park rules prohibit collecting wood within the park. Only three campgrounds, Black Rock, Indian Cove, and Cottonwood, have water—at all the others, campers must bring their own water. There are no showers and no hookups or dump stations for recreational vehicles, but such facilities are available in the towns near the park. In addition to the campgrounds, several day-use-only picnic areas are located in the park.

Black Rock Campground

This easy-to-reach campground is located south of Yucca Valley on Joshua Lane, near the mouth of Black Rock Canyon, and has 98 sites, drinking water, a horse camp, and a nature center. Because the campground is so close to the town of Yucca Valley, campers can easily go into town for supplies or meals during their camping trips. A nature trail and several longer trails make exploration of the area possible.

Indian Cove Campground

Popular both because of easy access and its spectacular setting in granite boulders at the northern end of the Wonderland of Rocks, this campground and picnic area is reached by turning south from Highway 62 between the towns of Joshua Tree and Twentynine Palms. The campground has 101 sites, drinking water, and a group area and is popular with rock climbers. A nature trail and several longer trails are nearby.

Hidden Valley Campground

Another campground popular with climbers, this campground with 40 sites is set amid granite boulders at the southwest corner of the Wonderland of Rocks along Park Boulevard. It can be reached from either the West or North Entrance. Water is not available. The Hidden Valley Nature Trail and Picnic Area is nearby, as are several trailheads.

Split Rock, a huge granite boulder split by a crack, marks the Split Rock Picnic Area.

Ryan Campground

A short spur road just east of the Keys View Road junction leads from Park Boulevard to this campground, which is set amid a small area of granite boulders in Lost Horse Valley. There are 31 sites, and water is not available. The Cap Rock Nature Trail and the California Hiking and Riding Trail are nearby, and there is a spur trail from the campground to the old Ryan Ranch site.

Sheep Pass Campground

This is a group site available by reservation only, located along Park Boulevard in Queen Valley. Water is not available.

Jumbo Rocks Campground

Another popular campground set among granite boulders, this large campground has 123 sites and is along Park Boulevard a few miles west of the Pinto Wye. There is no water. The Skull Rock Nature Trail loops through the campground, and the Live Oak and Split Rock Picnic Areas are nearby. There are a number of longer trails in the area, and the campground also makes a good base for exploring both the east and west portions of the park.

Belle Campground

This small campground located at the southwest corner of the Pinto Mountains along the Pinto Basin Road, about 2 miles south of the Pinto Wye, has 18 sites. Water is not available. Along with White Tank and Jumbo Rocks Campground, this centrally located campground makes a good base for exploring both the east and west portions of the park. The Twin Tanks Backcountry Board is nearby, which is a trailhead for the California Hiking and Riding Trail.

White Tank Campground

This small campground at the southwest corner of the Pinto Mountains along the Pinto Basin Road is about 4 miles south of the Pinto Wye. There are 15 sites, and water is not available. The Arch Rock Nature Trail starts here.

Cottonwood Campground

North of I–10 on Pinto Basin Road at the South Entrance, this campground has 62 sites, drinking water, a group site, a picnic area, and a nature trail. This is the perfect base from which to explore the eastern, Sonoran Desert section of the park.

An excellent loop scenic drive runs along Park Boulevard, starting at the Oasis Visitor Center just south of Highway 62 in Twentynine Palms and continuing west past the Pinto Wye to the West Entrance. Highway 62 can be used to complete the loop, which is 51 miles long. There are numerous pull-outs, as well several nature trails and picnic areas along Park Boulevard. A side road leads 5.5 miles one-way to Keys View and should not be missed.

The Pinto Basin Road starts from the Pinto Wye on Park Boulevard south of the North Entrance and leads 36.5 miles past the South Entrance and Cottonwood Visitor Center to I–10. This is a one-way scenic drive unless you use I–10 and other highways outside the park to make a loop. There are several nature trails and picnic areas along the road, as well as numerous pull-outs.

Both of these drives are described in detail below.

There are graded dirt roads, passable to ordinary cars, to Upper and Lower Covington Flats and Queen Valley. Other dirt roads, including the Geology Tour Road, Berdoo Canyon Road, Pinkham Canyon Road, Thermal Canyon Road, Black Eagle Mine Road, and Old Dale Road, are not maintained and require a four-wheel-drive vehicle. Off-road driving of any vehicle or bicycle is not permitted in the park.

One note of caution while driving in the park: Keep your speed down and observe posted limits. Roads are winding and intended for enjoyment of the scenery, not getting someplace fast. Never stop on the road; there are plenty of pull-outs at which to stop.

Park Boulevard Scenic Drive

Start from Oasis Visitor Center, which is an excellent place to become acquainted with the park. The visitor center has exhibits and displays, as well as a bookstore where you can also buy maps of the park. Park rangers on duty will be happy to answer any questions you may have.

From the Oasis Visitor Center, continue south on Utah Trail. The rugged desert mountains on your right rise like a wall from the desert plain along the road. After passing through the North Entrance Station, the road begins to wind a bit as it makes its way up the narrowing valley between the Pinto Mountains to the east and the Queen Mountain area to the west. After skirting the base of a rocky hill, the road curves right and passes the Pinto Basin Road turnoff. Stay right here and continue on Park Boulevard.

You'll soon come to a crossroads, where dirt roads lead both left and right. Turn right onto the short, graded dirt road to Split Rock. A small picnic area with restrooms is set below Split Rock itself. This massive granite boulder is broken by a huge crack, probably a weakness in the rock (called a joint) that became a crack when the formerly buried rock was exposed by erosion.

Back at Park Boulevard, cross the paved road and drive the short dirt road to Live Oak Picnic Area, which is named for the huge canyon live oak in the wash at the west end of the picnic area. Another attraction, which requires a short hike, is Ivanpah Tank, a water catchment built during the cattle ranching days. Ivanpah Tank is located south of the east end of the picnic area.

Continue west on Park Boulevard a short distance to Skull Rock, where you can park on either side of the road. Skull Rock is a large granite boulder marked by two cavities near the base that resemble eye sockets. This type of cavity is common in desert granite, and appears to be caused by chemical erosion from water collecting in minute pits. Skull Rock Nature Trail loops past Skull Rock, runs through nearby Jumbo Rocks Campground, and then returns along the north side of Park Boulevard. This very scenic and short trail is well worth doing.

Just west of Jumbo Rocks Campground, another crossroads marks the Geology Tour Road on the left. This unmaintained dirt road requires a four-wheel-drive vehicle. The road on the right is the Queen Valley Road, which is passable to ordinary cars. Continue west on Park Boulevard, which now passes through Queen Valley. This broad desert flat is partly surrounded by the Queen Mountains to the north. At Sheep Pass, Park Boulevard runs through a gap just north of Ryan Mountain, and you'll pass the Ryan Mountain Trailhead, which is on the left.

After Park Boulevard enters the vast expanse of Wild Horse Valley, you reach the Ryan Ranch Trailhead on the right. Here, a short, easy trail leads to the ruins of Ryan Ranch, located at the west base of Ryan Mountain.

Just past the Ryan Ranch Trailhead, turn left on the Keys View Road. This side road leads past Cap Rock Picnic Area. Cap Rock is named for the bill-like formation on the top of a granite boulder pile, and an easy nature trail loops past the rock.

Keys View Road ends at Keys View, the highest point in the park reachable by paved road. The stunning view takes in the broad sweep of the Coachella Valley below and the high peaks of the San Bernadino and San Gregorio Mountains to the west and southwest. After enjoying the view and the short nature trail, follow Keys View Road back to Park Boulevard and turn left to continue the loop.

Skull Rock, one of the park's most famous landmarks, marks the start of the Skull Rock Nature Trail.

At the north end of Lost Horse Valley, turn right on the road to Barker Dam. This short paved road leads to the trailhead for the Barker Dam Nature Trail, and skirts along the scenic southern edge of the Wonderland of Rocks. The dirt Queen Valley Road continues east from the Barker Dam Trailhead, but return the way you came to Park Boulevard.

Almost immediately after turning right on Park Boulevard, turn left into the Hidden Valley Picnic Area. Here, a short nature trail enters a beautiful, hidden valley surrounded by impressive granite formations.

Park Boulevard continues northwest past Quail Springs Picnic Area. The actual springs are miles away at the base of the Quail Mountains to the west, and, like most springs in the park, are not reliable.

After Quail Springs Picnic Area, Park Boulevard winds northwest through scenic granite formations and eventually leaves the park at the West Entrance. Drive north to Highway 62 in the town of Joshua Tree, and then turn right to continue the loop.

East of the town of Joshua Tree, turn right on Indian Cove Road. The cove is actually a sloping desert plain surrounded on the west, south, and north by granite formations of the Wonderland of Rocks. A picnic area is located east of the campground, in the mouth of Rattlesnake Canyon, and a nature trail starts from the end of the spur road west of the campground.

Return to Highway 62, and turn right to return to Twentynine Palms and the end of the loop drive.

Pinto Basin Scenic Drive

This drive starts from Pinto Wye on Park Boulevard and is most easily reached from the Oasis Visitor Center in Twentynine Palms by driving south on Utah Trail through the North Entrance. Alternatively, you can do the drive in reverse by starting from the Cottonwood Entrance off I–10 at the south side of the park.

A pair of small campgrounds are on the east side of the Pinto Basin Road just south of Pinto Wye. The second of these, White Tank Campground, has a nature trail that loops past a small natural arch, a rarity in granite.

Beyond the campgrounds, the Pinto Basin Road descends rapidly, soon leaving the higher-altitude Mojave Desert behind and entering the lower Sonoran Desert. After descending through Wilson Canyon, the road comes out into Pinto Basin, a broad desert plain flanked by the distant Pinto Mountains to the north and the Hexie Mountains to the south. A nature trail at Cholla Cactus Garden wanders through an especially dense patch of cholla cactus, while offering views of the distant mountains.

Pinto Basin Road swings around the east end of the Hexie Mountains and then heads generally southwest to the Cottonwood area. This complex contains a small visitor center as well as a ranger station, campground, and picnic area. Turn left on the Cottonwood Road and drive a short distance to the Cottonwood Spring Nature Trail. This short trail takes you to one of the few reliable springs in the park.

Cottonwood is the end of the Pinto Basin Scenic Drive. You can continue out of the park to the south to I–10, or retrace your way on Pinto Basin Road and Park Boulevard to Twentynine Palms.

Desert Wildflowers

Joshua Tree National Park is famous for its spring wildflower displays. At other times of the year, visitors may have a hard time believing that the seemingly barren desert can bring forth such an amazing variety and density of flowers. As described in the "Natural History" section, many desert plants survive long periods of drought in seed form. Millions of these seeds lie buried in the dusty desert soil, waiting for the right conditions.

Watch the Weather

Weather is the key. In order to germinate, these ephemeral plants need moisture in the form of fall and winter rains. Long, gentle rains are much better than sudden, heavy downpours, which tend to run off in flash floods. By January, if the rains have been sufficient, ephemeral plants will start to show up, especially at the lower elevations. But rainfall alone is not enough to trigger a spring flower show. Most of the plants need a period of warm, but not hot, late-winter temperatures in order to flower. So, the key weather to watch for is a series of gentle winter rains, followed by warm and dry late-winter and early-spring temperatures. Of course, once the scorching heat of summer arrives, the flowers quickly wilt and the plants die.

Where and When

At the lowest elevations of the park, along the south boundary and the Pinto Basin Road between I–10 and Cottonwood Visitor Center, flowers may bloom as early as February. At the highest elevations, flowers may still be blooming as late as June.

Desert star likes to grow nestled between granite boulders.

In the eastern, Sonoran Desert portion of the park, at elevations of 1,000 to 3,000 feet, annuals (ephemerals) tend to bloom from February through April. Yuccas favor March and April, while cacti appear somewhat later, March through June.

In the western, Mojave Desert section of the park, at elevations of 3,000 to 5,000 feet, the annuals tend to favor March through May, while the cacti bloom from April through June. Joshua trees tend to flower during March and April.

Check with the park visitor centers for updated information on flowering within the park. Another good source of information is www.desertusa.com, where individuals file reports and post photos of flowers throughout the desert Southwest.

Clear, dry desert air and the absence of lights from major cities create great conditions for observing the night sky from the park. The best time of the month for seeing the full richness of the night sky is during the new moon, but a partial moon can make it a bit easier to pick out the major constellations by washing out the myriad of dimmer stars.

Planets, being much closer to the Earth than any of the stars, change position in the night sky fairly rapidly. Those closest to the Earth, known as the major planets, are easily visible with the naked eye. Mercury, because it orbits close to the sun, is only visible in the twilight sky just after sunset or just before sunrise. Venus, the brightest object in the sky after the sun and moon, is often a spectacular white jewel in the evening or morning sky, blazing away well after sunset or before sunrise. Mars, the red planet, can be very bright during its closest approach to Earth. Jupiter and Saturn both shine brightly, despite their great distance from Earth, because of their huge sizes.

A pair of binoculars will bring out such details as the white, cloudy disk of Venus, the shades of red and orange of the Martian desert, the moons of Jupiter, and the rings of Saturn. With binoculars, you can also see such spectacular sights as Andromeda, the nearest galaxy to our own Milky Way, and other galaxies and nebulas.

Also, don't forget to watch for satellites. Many satellites, such as the International Space Station, are bright and easy to see. The best time to watch for satellites starts about an hour after sunset, when the sky is dark but sunlight still illuminates satellites in orbit.

A simple planisphere, a rotating disk that shows the night sky in correct orientation for the time of year and night, makes it easy to pick out the major stars and constellations. A good field guide is indispensable for those who want in-depth information on the night sky. See appendix A for recommendations. For current sky and planet data, as well as observing information on the space station, the Space Shuttle, and many other satellites, check out www.heavens-above.com.

Summer

Although the days are hot, desert nights tend to be cool and can be a great time to observe the sky. Use caution when moving around in the desert at night in the summer, because many creatures, including snakes and scorpions, are active at night. Use a flashlight, directed toward the ground with the beam partially hooded to avoid destroying your night vision.

During the evening, look south in the summer sky and you'll see the luminosity of the Milky Way, our home galaxy, rising from the southern horizon and arcing northeast across the sky. The Milky Way is a disk-shaped cloud of millions of stars. As you look south, you're looking at the disk of stars edge-wise. A bright red star not too far above the horizon is Antares, the red heart of Scorpius. The Scorpion is one of the largest and most distinctive constellations in the sky—the stinger is clearly visible, flipped back and ready to strike. Another large constellation up and to the left (or northeast) from Scorpius is Sagittarius, the Archer. A group of bright stars in Sagittarius looks like a teapot tilted to the right, ready to pour. Looking toward Sagittarius, you are actually looking toward the center of the Milky Way galaxy.

If you turn and look east, you'll see the Milky Way sweeping across the sky to dip below the northern horizon. Several very bright stars are in or near the Milky Way. Altair is a bright star in the constellation Aquila, which looks like a giant ice cream cone opening into the Milky Way. Deneb is a bright star that forms the top of the Northern Cross, a giant cross lying on its left side along the Milky Way. The Northern Cross is actually part of the constellation Cygnus, the Swan. Just to the southwest of Deneb, another very bright star is Vega, which is part of the constellation Lyra, the Lyre. This small constellation has six stars, including Vega, which form a triangle and a parallelogram with the corners joined.

Looking directly to the north, you can see Polaris, the North Star. Because Polaris is very near the celestial north pole, it appears to stay fixed in place all night, while all the other stars wheel around it. Polaris has been valuable to navigators from ancient times and is still useful to the desert adventurer today.

If you're having trouble finding Polaris, which is not as bright as Vega, look to the northwest for the Big Dipper. Part of the giant constellation Ursa Major, the Great Bear, the dipper appears to be hanging from its handle with the dipper opening to the right. The pair of stars making up the lower end of the dipper, nearest to the horizon, are called the Pointer Stars because a line drawn through them from left to right (south to north) points almost directly at Polaris. Below and right of Polaris is Cassiopeia, which forms a huge W lying on its side in the Milky Way.

In the western sky another famous constellation is about to set: Leo the Lion, marked by another bright star, Regulus. Leo is one of the twelve zodiac constellations that lie along the plane of the ecliptic, which is the path the planets, the moon, and the sun take across the night sky. If you hear an astronomer say that Mars is in Leo, he or she means that Mars is in the Leo portion of the zodiac.

Fall

The generally clear skies of fall in the California desert are nearly perfect for stargazing. By mid-October the teapot-shape of Sagittarius is still just visible above the southwest horizon.

To the east the Pleiades are a small cluster of stars looking like a tiny dipper just above the horizon. Technically, the Pleiades are an asterism, which is a named group of stars that is part of a larger, official constellation—in this case Taurus the Bull. Most of Taurus is still below the eastern horizon at 9:00 P.M. in mid-October, but if you're willing to stay up another hour, you'll see the distinctive V shape of Taurus rise, marked by a bright red star called Aldebaran.

To the north, Polaris hangs in its usual spot, but the Big Dipper is now below it, just above the northern horizon. Polaris forms the right end of the handle of the Little Dipper, part of Ursus Minor, the Little Bear. The Little Dipper is upside down and much smaller and fainter than the Big Dipper, with the bowl of the dipper to the left of Polaris.

In the western sky, Vega is now nearly overhead. Closer to the northwest horizon is a small semicircle of medium-bright stars, opening to the right and up. This is Corona Borealis, the Northern Crown.

Winter

Sirius, the Dog Star, dominates the winter night sky. This brilliant blue-white star is the brightest star in the sky, and in mid-January it hangs in the southeast, part of the constellation Canis Major, the Great Dog. Sirius is also one of the closest stars to our sun, lying "just" 52,000,000,000,000 miles away. Light from Sirius takes 8.7 years to reach Earth.

Orion the Hunter is probably the most distinctive constellation in the winter sky. Orion is a large rectangle of bright stars high in the southeast sky. The star at the upper left is Betelgeuse, a giant red star. In the middle of the rectangle, three bright stars in a close line are the Hunter's belt, while three more stars in a line below the belt are the Hunter's sword.

Early in the evening Leo the Lion is just rising in the east, while between Leo and Orion a pair of bright stars, Pollux and Castor, mark the constellation Gemini, the Twins. Procyon is the brightest star in the constellation Canis Minor, south of Gemini.

Looking north, the Little Dipper now dangles straight down from Polaris, and to the east the Big Dipper stands on its handle. Cassiopeia now forms a giant M tilted to the left, high above Polaris to the left.

To the west look for a large square of medium-bright stars standing on a corner. Known as the Great Square, this is the heart of the constellation Pegasus, the Winged Horse. The uppermost star is the bottom point of a cornucopia-shaped group of stars, which opens out upward and to the right, sweeping towards the Milky Way. This is the constellation Andromeda. Above the bottom star, three pairs of stars outline the curving form of Andromeda. If you look at the middle pair, and then look to the right, you may see a faint, fuzzy object. If you have any doubt, look at the area with binoculars. You should easily pick up a disk-shaped fuzzy object. You're looking at Andromeda galaxy, a swirling mass of millions of stars much like our own Milky Way galaxy, and the only object outside of our galaxy visible to the naked eye.

Spring .

Other than the Milky Way, the southern sky is fairly unremarkable in the spring. One exception is the bright star Spica, to the southeast in the constellation Virgo, the Virgin. Leo the Lion is almost directly overhead in the evening.

Looking eastward you'll spot a bright red star well above the horizon. This is Arcturus in the constellation Bootes. Bootes looks like a giant ice cream cone lying on its left side. Vega, in Lyra, has been absent from the evening sky all winter, but if you stay up a couple of hours after dark, you'll see it rise in the northeast.

In the northern sky the Big Dipper is now upside down and high above Polaris. The W shape of Cassiopeia is very close to the horizon, and a bright red star, Capella, glows to the northwest in the constellation Auriga.

To the west Orion lies low above the horizon, flanked by Sirius the Dog Star to the left, and the distinctive small V of stars in Taurus, with bright red Aldebaran at the upper left. High above Orion, the twin stars in Gemini mark the zodiac, while Capella shines brightly in Canis Minor to the south.

Bicycling the Park

Bicycles are allowed on all roads in the park but not on trails. A new park-management plan under development would allow bicycles on some of the trails outside the wilderness portion of the park. Check with a park ranger or at one of the visitor centers for the current status.

Because water sources are far between, cyclists must carry plenty of water. During the hot summer months, the best riding time is between sunrise and midmorning. Even during the cool months, you'll lose plenty of moisture riding in the dry desert air, so don't underestimate the amount of water you'll need. Always wear a helmet. If you are unfamiliar with the environment and riding conditions, start off with short rides and work up to longer ones.

Road Rides

Both Pinto Basin Road and Park Boulevard are paved and wind through spectacular scenery. See "Scenic Drives" for a detailed description of both roads. All the paved park roads are narrow and winding, with soft shoulders. During the peak seasons, there will be a lot of car traffic, so use caution.

From the Oasis Visitor Center to the West Entrance, there is more than 2,800 feet of elevation gain over 29.1 miles. The only water is at Oasis Visitor Center. The best way to do this ride is with a shuttle, starting at the West Entrance and ending at Oasis Visitor Center.

Pinto Basin Road climbs 2,300 feet in 29.6 miles from Cottonwood Visitor Center to Pinto Wye. The only water is found at Cottonwood Visitor Center. A good way to do this ride is with a shuttle, starting from Pinto Wye and ending at the Cottonwood Visitor Center.

Those looking for an easier road ride could do just a portion of Park Boulevard, starting at one of the many picnic areas or campgrounds along the road. Another easy ride is the paved Indian Cove Road, starting from the Indian Cove Entrance and riding to Indian Cove Picnic Area and return. The round-trip distance is 6 miles and the elevation gain is 300 feet.

Mountain Bike Rides

Although there is no single track in the park at present, some of the dirt roads are excellent rides. Better riding conditions are found on the graded dirt roads.

Unmaintained double track roads, such as the Geology Tour Road, and Old Dale and Black Eagle Mine Roads, tend to be sandy and offer tough going.

The Queen Valley Road, which becomes a graded dirt road at the Barker Dam Trailhead, is a scenic ride through Queen Valley along the south side of the Wonderland of Rocks and Queen Mountains to the Pine City Trailhead and back. The round-trip distance is 7.2 miles, with little elevation gain.

Another interesting ride starts from the junction of the Lower and Upper Covington Flat Roads in Lower Covington Flat. You can ride the Upper Covington Flat Road and the Eureka Peak Road to the summit of Eureka Peak and back, a round-trip distance of 5.8 miles and a climb of 700 feet. Eureka Peak offers a spectacular view of the western portion of the park, as well as the San Jacinto and San Gregorio Mountains to the west. A worthwhile side trip takes you to the Upper Covington Trailhead, where you'll ride among some of the largest Joshua trees in the park. This side road adds 3.4 miles and 300 feet of elevation gain to the ride. All these roads are double track.

Rock Climbing

Joshua Tree National Park is a very popular rock climbing area, with more than 4,500 established, named routes. Although the granite formations of the park lack the high faces of places such as Yosemite Valley and Tahquitz Rock, J-Tree, as climbers call it, more than makes up for the lack of long climbs with an astonishing variety of small faces, cracks, and giant boulders. It is literally a wonderland of rock climbing.

Because some of the most popular climbing areas are near the main park roads, picnic areas, and campgrounds, you'll almost certainly see rock climbers in action, especially during the spring. If you're not a climber, read on for an introduction to the sport as practiced at J-Tree. If you are a climber, then refer to appendix A for a list of useful guidebooks.

Why Climb?

To the uninitiated, rock climbing looks extremely dangerous. It is true that defying gravity can have serious consequences, just as in other activities involving the vertical dimension, such as flying. However, modern climbing technique and equipment make the risk almost completely manageable. Like that of any other modern sport, rock climbing technique has been developed and refined over many years. After gaining some experience, rock climbers ascend in complete control on tiny holds and up vertical cracks, always knowing where their limits are. The only time rock climbers are likely to fall is when they push their limits to overcome a climbing problem at the limit of their skill.

Another popular activity, especially in Joshua Tree, is bouldering. This involves working out routes on boulders high enough to offer a series of interesting moves but too small to establish a climbing route. Sometimes boulderers are protected by ropes, but more often they lay out a portable, cushioned mat below the boulder and depend on another climber to spot them if they fall.

Learning to Climb

Rock climbing is not a sport you can learn from books. The safest way to learn is with a climbing school, either a commercial service or a school put on by a climbing club. Most large cities have active climbing clubs, and the members can often recommend good commercial climbing schools as well.

Rock climbing is popular throughout the park.

Popular Climbing Areas

Indian Cove is an extremely popular area, due to its accessibility. There are many routes that start right out of sites in the Indian Cove Campground, which is why you'll see a lot of climbers camped there.

Another popular area is Hidden Valley Campground. In the spring it's difficult to find a site not occupied by climbers. Not only are there many routes in the campground, the campground is also a jumping-off area for the many routes found in the nearby Wonderland of Rocks.

People walking the Cap Rock Nature Trail are very likely to see climbers on Cap Rock itself, as well as the neighboring rocks. Nearby Ryan Campground has some classic routes on the formations in the campground.

Jumbo Rocks Campground offers a great deal of climbing, not only on the formations in the campground itself but also in the areas to the north and east. The Split Rock and Live Oak areas further east are also popular.

Most of the trailheads in the park are located along the park's main access roads, Park Boulevard and the Pinto Basin Road, and are accessible to ordinary cars. Approaches to these trailheads are described starting from Highway 62 in Joshua Tree for trails nearer to the West Entrance, from Highway 62 in Twentynine Palms for trailheads closer to the North Entrance, or from Interstate 10 for the trailheads along the southern section of the Pinto Basin Road. Several trailheads are located on dead-end roads leading south from Highway 62; these include Black Rock Canyon, Upper and Lower Covington Flats, Indian Cove, and Fortynine Palms Oasis. Approaches to these trailheads are described starting from Highway 62 between Twentynine Palms and Yucca Valley. Most of the remaining trails start from the Pinto Basin Road; these approaches are described starting at I–10 and the Pinto Basin Road.

Since all hikers wishing to spend a night or more in the backcountry must register at a backcountry board, it is helpful to know their location. (All are shown on the four-color map included with this book.) Backcountry boards are located at the entrance to Black Rock Campground, in Upper Covington Flat, and just south of Indian Cove park entrance. Along Park Boulevard, backcountry boards are located at Keys West, just east of Quail Springs Picnic Area, at Juniper Flat on the Keys View Road just south of Park Boulevard, at Pine City Trailhead on the Desert Queen Mine Road north of Park Boulevard, and just south of the North Entrance Station. The Geology Tour and Pleasant Valley Backcountry Boards are located on the four-wheel-drive Geology Tour Road. Twin Tanks, Turkey Flats, and Porcupine Wash backcountry boards are found along the Pinto Basin Road. The Cottonwood Spring Backcountry Board is located at the Cottonwood Spring Trailhead at the south end of the Pinto Basin Road. There are no backcountry boards or marked trailheads in the remote eastern portion of the park, which is accessible mainly from the four-wheel-drive Black Eagle Mine and Old Dale Roads, off Pinto Basin Road, or from Highways 62 and 177 on the north and east sides of the park.

Mileages

Trail mileages are for the total distance of a hike. For one-way hikes, which require a car shuttle, the total distance assumes you will actually leave a shuttle

Arch Rock, a rare granite natural arch, is located along the Arch Rock Nature Trail in White Tank Campground.

vehicle at the end of the hike and do it one-way. Loop-hook mileages were carefully measured with topographic mapping software. This was done for consistency, so that while the book's mileages may not always agree with official distances or trail signs, you can confidently compare hikes within the book.

Difficulty Ratings

All hikes are described as easy, moderate, or strenuous, a highly subjective rating that nevertheless should help you decide which hikes are for you. Generally, easy hikes are fairly short, can be done in an hour or two, and have little elevation change. A few of these hikes are on smooth or paved trails that are wheelchair-accessible. Moderate hikes are longer, take up to half a day or so, often have significant elevation change, and may have sections of cross-country hiking, so you should be in reasonable shape for hiking and have good footwear and a pack to carry water and other essentials. Strenuous hikes are long and take most of a day or several days, almost always have large elevation changes, and may be all or partially cross-country. Remember that trail conditions can change because of storms, wildfires, or just plain lack of use and maintenance. Check with the Park Service for the latest information on trail conditions.

Route Finding

Don't depend on trail signs for finding your way: Signs are often missing and sometimes inaccurate. While most of the trails described in this book were chosen because they are well used and easy to follow, there are many official trails shown on maps that are faint and receive little maintenance, as well as informal trails created by other hikers who may or may not know where they are going. Cairned routes, marked by piles of rock, should be followed with a healthy skepticism. Cairns are often constructed casually, with no thought to the overall route, and even by lost hikers. On cross-country routes, you should have a topographic map.

In Joshua Tree National Park, many land features, such as washes, canyons, ridges, and summits, do not have official names. In the case of unnamed peaks, this guide uses the elevation shown on the USGS topographic map as a name. Be responsible for your own route finding—don't leave it to others. Use a good map and keep track of your location as you go. Tracking your location on a map also helps you judge your rate of progress, so you know when to turn back or when you'll arrive at a spring or planned campsite. And always carry a high-quality compass, even if you bring a GPS unit.

The Maps

A park brochure map is available at the entrance stations and both visitor centers. However, you'll find a FalconGuide four-color foldout map at the back of this book. The front side of our map offers an overview of the entire national park with an accompanying map legend and hypsometric key. The reverse side includes detail maps that show selected areas of the park.

In the accompanying FalconGuide maps, all trail positioning has been verified using topo maps and the latest information for the greatest possible accuracy. Our maps also contain more detail, such as topography that shows both land and water features with the land elevation measured in feet. In addition, you'll find numerous activity icons on the maps highlighting the visitor centers, hiking trails, and overlooks. Campgrounds, backcountry campsites, and picnic areas are also depicted on the maps.

A few notes about reading the topography: All of our maps use shaded, or shadow, relief. Shadow relief does not represent elevation: It demonstrates slope or relative steepness. This gives an almost 3-D perspective of the physical geography of a region and will help you see where the ranges and valleys are.

All our maps employ a technique called *hypsometry*, which uses elevation tints to portray relief. Each tone represents a range of equal elevation, as shown in the hypsometric key on the map. These maps will give you a good idea of elevation gain and loss. The color tones shown on the bottom of the key represent lower elevations while the tones toward the top represent higher elevations. Narrow bands of different tones spaced closely together indicate steep terrain, whereas wider bands indicate areas of more gradual slope.

If you'd like to supplement our map with a more detailed map for backcountry travel, you may want to obtain the 7.5-minute series of topographic maps published by the U.S. Geological Survey (USGS). Electronic versions of these maps can be found online or as packaged software. USGS maps are derived from aerial photos and are extremely accurate when it comes to terrain and natural features, but because the *topos*, as they are known, are not revised very often, trail, road, and other man-made features are often out of date. Even so, the 7.5-minute topo's fine depiction of topography is useful for seeing greater detail.

Share the Trail

Some of the trails in this book are open to horseback riders as well as hikers. Mountain bikes are not allowed on wilderness trails but may be encountered on certain designated trails and on roads. The park's paved roads are popular with road cyclists as well. Horses always have the right of way over hikers and cyclists, both of which should move off the trail or dirt road downhill and remain still until the horses have passed. Talking quietly to the riders helps convince the horses that you are a person and not some weird monster with a hump on its back. Don't make sudden movements or noises.

Technically, hikers have the right of way over cyclists, but in practice it's more reasonable for hikers to step off the trail so as to avoid forcing the riders off road. On their part, cyclists should be courteous, always ride under control, and warn hikers and equestrians of their approach.

Black Rock Canyon Area

South Park Peak

This short nature trail located just outside Joshua Tree National Park loops over a 4,395-foot peak with sweeping views of the Black Rock Canyon area and Yucca Valley. The 0.7-mile hike is easy. Interpretive signs along the trail explain desert plants and wildlife. There is a picnic area at the trailhead.

FINDING THE TRAILHEAD: From the intersection of Highway 62 and Joshua Lane in Yucca Valley, go south on Joshua Lane for 5 miles. Before reaching the Joshua Tree National Park boundary, turn right on a dirt road and continue 0.6 mile to the trailhead and picnic area.

MAPS: Yucca Valley South USGS.

High View Nature Trail

This easy 1.2-mile interpretive nature trail starts from the South Park Peak Trailhead and loops south into the foothills west of the campground. Numbered posts are indexed to a brochure available from the Black Rock Visitor Center, which explains plant and animal adaptation to the desert. There is a picnic area at the trailhead.

FINDING THE TRAILHEAD: From the intersection of Highway 62 and Joshua Lane in Yucca Valley, go south on Joshua Lane for 5 miles. Before reaching the Joshua Tree National Park boundary, turn right on a dirt road and continue 0.6 mile to the trailhead and picnic area. This trail can also be reached by a 0.4-mile spur trail from the ranger station in Black Rock Campground.

MAPS: Yucca Valley South USGS.

Panorama Loop

This aptly named 5.7-mile hike takes you over several peaks with views of the west end of Joshua Tree National Park as well as the Salton Sea, Mount San Jacinto, and Mount San Gorgonio. This is a moderately difficult hike. During the hot summer months, plan to hike early in the day and carry plenty of water.

A tall Joshua tree stands sentinel along the Black Rock Canyon Trail above Black Rock Canyon Campground.

FINDING THE TRAILHEAD: From the intersection of Highway 62 and Joshua Lane in Yucca Valley, go south on Joshua Lane 5.1 miles to the Black Rock Backcountry Board.

MAP: Yucca Valley South USGS.

THE HIKE: From the Black Rock Backcountry Board, follow the trail up Black Rock Wash. This broad, sandy wash is popular with horses, and the going may be slow in soft sand. Stay right at the junction with the California Riding and Hiking Trail, remaining in Black Rock Wash. At 0.7 mile stay left where the trail forks right to the south end of Black Rock Campground, a good alternative start and finish for those hikers staying in the campground. (Use care at a water tank to stay on the trail.)

As you continue up Black Rock Wash, the trail reaches the base of the foothills, and at 1.4 mile you'll pass Black Rock Spring, which is usually dry. Just 0.2 mile beyond the spring, the wash forks; turn left to start the loop portion of the hike. Continue east-southeast up this wash to its head, where a trail leads south to Peak 5,195 at 2.7 miles.

From the summit, the trail heads southwest down a ridge, then turns west to return to Black Rock Wash. Follow the wash downstream, past the loop junction and Black Rock Spring, to the Black Rock Trailhead.

Eureka Peak

This long out-and-back hike to 5,518-foot Eureka Peak is 8.2 miles long and strenuous. Black Rock Campground and a horse camp are nearby. During the hot summer months, plan to hike early in the day and carry plenty of water.

FINDING THE TRAILHEAD: From the intersection of Highway 62 and Joshua Lane in Yucca Valley, go south on Joshua Lane for 5.1 miles to the Black Rock Backcountry Board.

MAPS: Yucca Valley South, Joshua Tree South USGS.

THE HIKE: From the Black Rock Trailhead, follow the California Riding and Hiking Trail east-southeast across the desert foothills. After about 1.3 miles, the trail meets a fork in a wash. The trail continues east-southeast up the left fork of the wash, but the route up Eureka Peak turns right and heads south up the right fork of the wash. Continue up the wash, which is marked with posts labeled EP, to its head, then follow the route marked with EP posts to the ridge just south of Eureka Peak. (The park plans to replace these EP posts with trail signs.) Here you are on the 0.2-mile trail from the Upper Covington Flat Road to Eureka Peak. Turn left and walk 0.1 mile to the summit. Retrace your steps back to the trailhead.

CALIFORNIA RIDING
AND HIKING TRAIL

↑
COVINGTON FLATS   7.6 MI
KEYS VIEW ROAD   18.9 MI
RYAN CAMPGROUND   19.7 MI
GEOLOGY TOUR ROAD   25.5 MI
PINTO BASIN ROAD   30.0 MI
NORTH TRAILHEAD   37.3 MI

Crossing the park from west to east, the California Riding and Hiking Trail is open to equestrians and hikers.

Burnt Hill Loop

This moderately difficult 5.8-mile hike loops up through an old burn area in the foothills above Black Rock Wash, using part of the Eureka Peak route for the return. Black Rock Campground and a horse camp are nearby. During the hot summer months, plan to hike early in the day and carry plenty of water.

FINDING THE TRAILHEAD: From the intersection of Highway 62 and Joshua Lane in Yucca Valley, go south on Joshua Lane for 5.1 miles to the Black Rock Backcountry Board.

MAPS: Yucca Valley South, Joshua Tree South USGS.

THE HIKE: From the Black Rock Trailhead, hike south on the Black Rock Wash Trail for 0.5 mile, then turn left on the Burnt Hill Trail, which is marked with posts labeled BH. The trail climbs southeast over a pass at mile 2.6, then turns east to meet the route up Eureka Peak in a wash. Turn left at mile 2.9, and hike down the wash to the north (marked with posts labeled EP). At a fork in the wash, you'll meet the California Riding and Hiking Trail. Turn left and follow the California Riding and Hiking Trail back to the Black Rock Trailhead.

Covington Flats Area

Covington Loop

This is a moderately difficult 3.8-mile cross-country loop that passes through a rugged canyon. During the hot summer months, plan to hike early in the day and carry plenty of water.

FINDING THE TRAILHEAD: From the intersection of Highway 62 and La Contenta Road in Yucca Valley, drive south on La Contenta Road, which becomes the Covington Flat Road and enters the park. At 8.6 miles turn right on the Upper Covington Flat Road. After 0.7 mile turn left at the Eureka Peak Road and follow the Upper Covington Flat Road to its end at the Upper Covington Backcountry Board.

MAPS: Joshua Tree South USGS.

THE HIKE: From the Upper Covington Trailhead, walk a few yards southeast on the California Riding and Hiking Trail to the point where it crosses a wash. Leave the trail and head northeast down the wash, which soon enters the upper portion of Smith Water Canyon. After the wash emerges from the canyon at

A seasonal creek creates braided stream channels in upper Smith Water Canyon.

mile 1.3, it crosses the Lower Covington Flat Trail southeast of the Lower Covington Picnic Area. Turn right on the Lower Covington Flat Trail and follow it 1 mile to the California Riding and Hiking Trail at mile 2.3. Turn right and follow the California Riding and Hiking Trail west to the Upper Covington Trailhead. The last section of the trail passes through a portion of Upper Covington Flat with some of the largest Joshua trees in the entire park.

Indian Cove Area

Indian Cove Nature Trail

This easy 0.6-mile loop nature trail wanders through the foothills near large granite boulders and formations. The trailhead is at the west end of Indian Cove Campground. There is a picnic area east of the campground.

FINDING THE TRAILHEAD: From Highway 62 at Indian Cove Road west of Twentynine Palms, drive south on Indian Cove Road to Indian Cove Campground. Bear right through the campground to reach the Indian Cove Nature Trail parking area at the west end of the campground, 3.8 miles from Highway 62.

MAPS: Indian Cove USGS.

THE HIKE: From the parking area, the trail heads west and drops into a wash, then follows the wash northeast before turning south to return to the trailhead. Interpretive signs explain common desert plants and animals.

Fortynine Palms Oasis

One of five palm oases in the park, this spring lies in a rugged canyon on the north side of the park. The entire 2.6-mile out-and-back hike is in a day-use area and is moderately difficult. There is a paved parking area and restrooms. During the hot summer months, plan to hike early in the day and carry plenty of water.

FINDING THE TRAILHEAD: From the intersection of Highway 62 and Canyon Road west of Twentynine Palms, turn south on Canyon road and drive 1.5 miles to the end of the road and Fortynine Palms Trailhead.

MAPS: Queen Mountain USGS.

California fan palms mark Fortynine Palms Oasis, one of several oases, or springs, in the park.

THE HIKE: The well-used trail climbs over a ridge studded with small barrel cacti, then descends into a north-draining canyon. You'll spot the palms well before you reach them. Several fires have burned the palms over the years, blackening the trunks but not otherwise harming them. The huge granite boulders, deep shade, trickling water, and bird calls complete this very pleasant setting. Retrace your steps to return to the trailhead.

Hidden Valley Area

Quail Springs Trail

This 7.8-mile out-and-back hike through an open valley with plenty of Joshua trees leads to a seasonal spring. The trailhead is at the Quail Springs Picnic Area. The trail is moderately difficult and open to horseback riding. During the hot summer months, plan to hike early in the day and carry plenty of water.

> **FINDING THE TRAILHEAD:** From Highway 62 in Joshua Tree, go 11.2 miles south and southeast on Quail Spring Road/Park Boulevard to the Quail Springs Picnic Area.
> **MAPS:** Indian Cove, Joshua Tree South USGS.

THE HIKE: From the Quail Springs Picnic Area, head west on the Quail Springs Trail, which follows an old road along the north base of the mountains. Stay right at the junction with the trail into Johnny Lang Canyon at mile 1.9. After passing the junction the trail continues west into the canyon at the head of Quail Wash, then turns south to end at Quail Springs at the base of the hills. Retrace your steps to return to the trailhead.

Willow Hole

This is a popular trail and cross-country hike to an area of seasonal pools in the Wonderland of Rocks. The 7-mile out-and-back hike is moderately difficult; horseback riding is permitted. Willow Hole and most of the Wonderland of Rocks is in a day-use area. Parking and facilities are available at Keys West Backcountry Board. During the hot summer months, plan to hike early in the day and carry plenty of water.

FINDING THE TRAILHEAD: The trailhead is located at the Keys West Backcountry Board. To reach this trailhead from Highway 62 in Joshua Tree, drive 11.7 miles south and southeast on Quail Spring Road/Park Boulevard.

MAPS: Indian Cove USGS.

THE HIKE: The first portion of this hike follows the Boy Scout Trail, but at 1.3 miles you'll turn right onto the Willow Hole Trail. Follow the trail northeast across the desert flat. As the granite hills of the Wonderland of Rocks closes in around you, the trail meets and follows a dry tributary of Rattlesnake Canyon. After the wash veers sharply southeast, the trail ends at mile 2.8. Hike cross-country down the wash for 0.7 miles to Willow Hole, an area of seasonal pools and lush vegetation in the heart of the Wonderland of Rocks. Retrace your steps to return to the trailhead.

Hidden Valley Nature Trail

This scenic nature trail enters a valley hidden in huge granite boulders and loops around the perimeter. The easy 0.9-mile loop begins at the Hidden Valley Picnic Area.

FINDING THE TRAILHEAD: From Highway 62 in Joshua Tree, drive 14 miles south and southeast on Quail Spring Road/Park Boulevard, then turn right into the Hidden Valley Picnic Area.

MAPS: Indian Cove USGS.

THE HIKE: A few hundred yards of trail lead through a narrow gap in the rocks, emerging into a charming valley hidden among the granite rocks and cliffs. The clockwise loop starts at a sign, and interpretive signs explain the plants, animals, and geology of this interesting area.

Barker Dam Nature Trail

A scenic nature trail that loops through the Wonderland of Rocks to a small man-made lake, this easy hike is 1.2 miles long. The trail can also be hiked via two spur trails from Hidden Valley Campground.

A tiny seasonal creek is tucked away in Hidden Valley.

FINDING THE TRAILHEAD: From Highway 62 in Joshua Tree, drive 14 miles south and southeast on Quail Spring Road/Park Boulevard, then turn left on the Queen Valley Road. Continue 1.4 miles to the Barker Dam Trailhead and parking area, on the left.

MAPS: Indian Cove USGS.

THE HIKE: The trail almost immediately enters the Wonderland of Rocks, wandering between picturesque granite boulders. Interpretive signs explain the history and natural history of the area. After 0.2 mile the loop trail starts; stay right. Barker Dam was built by early ranchers to water cattle and then was improved by Bill Keys. It creates the largest pond in the park when full. The incongruity of this lake in such an arid setting underscores the fact that the most precious resource in the desert is water, far surpassing the long-term value of precious metals.

The loop trail continues along the shore past the dam, then turns west. As the trail heads south through a desert flat, you'll cross an informal access trail for rock climbers. Next, a spur goes right to Hidden Valley Campground. An interesting petroglyph site lies a short distance down this spur trail. Back on the main Barker Dam Nature trail, a last junction marks the end of the loop; turn right to return to the trailhead.

Wonderland Wash

A cross-country walk into the heart of the Wonderland of Rocks, this easy hike is 3.6 miles out and back. Wonderland Wash and most of the Wonderland of Rocks is in a day-use area. During the hot summer months, carry plenty of water and plan to hike early in the day. A paved parking lot with toilets is available.

FINDING THE TRAILHEAD: From Highway 62 in Joshua Tree, drive 14 miles south and southeast on Quail Spring Road/Park Boulevard, then turn left on the Queen Valley Road. Continue 1.5 miles to the Wall Street Mill Trailhead, on the left.

MAPS: Indian Cove USGS.

THE HIKE: Starting at the Wall Street Trailhead, walk the Wall Street Mill Trail 0.2 miles to the unsigned Wonderland Ranch Trail, an old road. Turn left and follow the trail 0.1 mile to the ruins of the pink ranch building. Walk a few yards northwest of the old ranch house to Wonderland Wash, and follow the wash upstream to the north approximately 1.4 miles to an area of large granite domes, some of which are 300 feet high. This area is popular with rock climbers.

Wall Street Mill

This pleasant walk to the ruins of a mining mill site at the edge of the Wonderland of Rocks is an easy out-and-back hike of 2 miles. Wall Street Mill and most of the Wonderland of Rocks are in a day-use area. A paved parking area with toilets is available.

FINDING THE TRAILHEAD: From Highway 62 in Joshua Tree, drive 14 miles south and southeast on Quail Spring Road/Park Boulevard, then turn left on the Queen Valley Road. Continue 1.5 miles to the Wall Street Mill Trailhead, on the left. (You can also start the hike at the Barker Dam Nature Trail Trailhead—this alternative is not described here.)

MAPS: Hidden Cove USGS.

THE HIKE: From the parking area, head northeast on the Wall Street Mill Trail. After 0.3 miles, an unsigned trail forks left to the ruins of Wonderland Ranch, which is visible through the Joshua trees. Stay right and continue on the Wall Street Mill Trail. Another unsigned trail forks left to the ruins of an old car at the base of the rocks; again, stay right. A wrecked windmill marks the sight of the Desert Queen Well. Windmills and their associated storage tanks and watering troughs such as this one were once a common sight in the desert West. Another half mile of walking leads to the ruins of Wall Street Mill, next to a wash. On the way you'll pass a granite marker where local resident Bill Keys shot and killed Worth Bagley. Bagley and Keys disputed the use of the road, and Bagley threatened Keys with a gun. The court found Keys guilty of murder, but after well-known author Earl Stanley Gardener researched his case with his "Court of Last Resort," a group of lawyers who helped out less fortunate cases, Keys received a full pardon. He was released from prison after serving five years.

Mills were used to smash and grind rock ore, so that the valuable minerals could be separated out.

Lost Horse Valley Area

Cap Rock Nature Trail

A short loop trail through granite boulders with great views of the surrounding area, this easy hike is only 0.4 mile long. There's a dirt parking area with picnic tables and toilets.

> **FINDING THE TRAILHEAD:** From Highway 62 in Joshua Tree, drive 15.8 miles south and southeast on Quail Spring Road/Park Boulevard, then turn right on Keys View Road. Go 0.1 mile and turn left into the Cap Rock Trailhead.
> **MAPS:** Keys View USGS.

THE HIKE: Cap Rock is the large granite dome north of the parking area. A small, visor-shaped rock perched on the top gave the formation its name. The trail loops around numerous granite boulders and squeezes through a narrow crack at one point. Interpretive trails identify and explain desert features, and this short but interesting trail offers great views of the surrounding Lost Horse Valley area and Ryan Mountain to the east.

The Cap Rock area is popular with rock climbers, who can often be seen working their way up the steep faces of the granite domes.

Ryan Ranch

This easy 1-mile hike along the foothills of Ryan Mountain leads to the ruins of an old ranch and back again. A paved parking area with toilets is available.

> **FINDING THE TRAILHEAD:** From Highway 62 in Joshua Tree, drive 16.2 miles south and southeast on Quail Spring Road/Park Boulevard to the Ryan Ranch Trailhead, on the right.
> **MAPS:** Keys View USGS.

THE HIKE: From the trailhead, this easy trail heads southeast across the Joshua tree flat east of Ryan Campground. At 0.4 mile a spur trail leads west to the campground; turn left here and follow the Ryan Ranch Trail another 0.1 mile to the ruins of Ryan Ranch. The steep slopes of Ryan Mountain form a rugged backdrop for the site.

Ryan Ranch is reached by an easy trail.

Ryan Mountain

This 2.4-mile out-and-back hike of moderate difficulty climbs to the top of 5,457-foot Ryan Mountain, which offers panoramic views of the central portion of the park, including Lost Horse and Queen Valleys and the Wonderland of Rocks to the north. During the hot summer months, plan to hike early in the day and carry plenty of water.

FINDING THE TRAILHEAD: From Highway 62 in Joshua Tree, drive 17.7 miles south and southeast on Quail Spring Road/Park Boulevard to the Ryan Mountain Trailhead on the right.

MAPS: Keys View USGS.

THE HIKE: From the trailhead, the Ryan Mountain Trail heads south to the base of the mountain, passing the spur trail to Sheep Pass Group Campground,

Ryan Mountain has a trail to the summit. It is seen here from the Cap Rock Nature Trail.

which joins from the left. A steady 1-mile ascent leads to the top of the peak and its stunning views of much of the central portion of the park.

Lost Horse Mine

This scenic 5.8-mile trail of moderate difficulty offers great views of Lost Horse Valley and loops over Lost Horse Mountain and past Lost Horse Mine. During the hot summer months, plan to hike early in the day and carry plenty of water. Horses are permitted on the trail.

FINDING THE TRAILHEAD: From Highway 62 in Joshua Tree, drive 15.8 miles south and southeast on Quail Spring Road/Park Boulevard, then turn right on Keys View Road. Continue 2.3 miles, then turn left on dirt Lost Horse Road. Continue 0.9 mile to the end of the road and the Lost Horse Mine Trailhead.

MAPS: Keys View USGS.

THE HIKE: From the trailhead, the Lost Horse Mine Trail initially heads east, but then turns generally southeast as it follows an old mining road to the top of Lost Horse Mountain. Just before climbing through a saddle at the trail's high point, a short spur trail leads northeast to the Lost Horse Mine and the top of the mountain. Views include Lost Horse Valley to the north, Keys View and Inspiration Peak to the west, and Pleasant Valley to the east.

Lost Horse Mine is the largest remaining historic mining area in the park. Exploration of the area reveals a ten-stamp mill, the ruins of several rock buildings, a deep, grated mineshaft, and a winch used to lower miners into a shaft. The first discovery in the Lost Horse area was made by a German miner, Frank Diebold. Later, in 1893, Johnny Lang, who was looking for a lost horse, happened on the claim and ended up buying it from Diebold. Extracting gold from such a mine involved several steps. First, of course, the gold-bearing rock had to be blasted, picked, and carried from the mine shafts. Then the ore was crushed to small particles in a mill. Next, the miners mixed mercury with the ore. Gold bonded with the mercury, which, being a liquid, could easily be separated from the crushed rock.

To continue the loop, follow the Lost Horse Mine Trail southeast down a ridge, then southwest to the foot of the mountain. Here the trail heads northwest and follows a wash back to the Lost Horse Mine Trailhead.

Keys View

This short (0.2 miles) but very scenic nature trail leads to the highest point reachable by paved road in the park. It's an easy, wheelchair-accessible loop hike, and there's a paved parking area with toilets.

FINDING THE TRAILHEAD: From Highway 62 in Joshua Tree, drive 15.8 miles south and southeast on Quail Spring Road/Park Boulevard, then turn right on Keys View Road. Continue 5.4 miles to the end of the road at Keys View.

MAPS: Keys View USGS.

Snowcapped San Jacinto and San Gorgonio Peaks form the western skyline from the wheelchair-accessible Keys View Trail.

THE HIKE: The paved Keys View Nature Trail starts from the Keys View parking lot and offers sweeping views of the Coachella Valley, the Palm Springs area, and San Jacinto Mountain to the southwest. Interpretive signs explain the major features of the view, including the trace of the San Andreas Fault, visible as a low bluff in the Coachella Valley. The trail is wheelchair-accessible from a handicap-only parking area just east of the main parking lot.

Inspiration Peak

This moderately difficult cross-country hike to 5,550-foot Inspiration Peak is 1.6 miles out and back. Located in a day-use area, Inspiration Peak has a paved parking area with toilets.

FINDING THE TRAILHEAD: From Highway 62 in Joshua Tree, drive 15.8 miles south and southeast on Quail Spring Road/Park Boulevard, then turn right on Keys View Road. Continue 5.4 miles to the end of the road at Keys View.

MAPS: Keys View USGS.

THE HIKE: From the Keys View parking area, hike cross-country up the ridge to the northeast. You'll hike over two false summits before making the final ascent to Inspiration Peak. Your reward for making the ascent is a 360-degree view of the southwest portion of Joshua Tree National Park.

Queen Valley Area

Negro Hill

From a dirt trailhead, this easy cross-country out-and-back 1-mile hike climbs to a high point that offers great views of the Queen Valley and surrounding mountains.

FINDING THE TRAILHEAD: From Highway 62 in Twentynine Palms, drive 13.7 miles south and west on Utah Trail/Park Boulevard to the east end of the Queen Valley Road. Turn right on this graded dirt road and drive 1.3 miles to the Pine City Backcountry Board.

MAPS: Queen Mountain USGS.

THE HIKE: From the Pine City Trailhead, hike west-northwest, cross-country, across the desert flats toward Negro Hill, then directly up the east slopes to the rounded summit. Though low, at 4,875 feet, Negro Hill offers a unique vantage point for viewing the Queen Valley from its isolated location.

Pine City

From a dirt trailhead, this is an easy 2.8-mile walk to the site of a former mining town and back. The site of Pine City is in a day-use area. During the hot summer months, plan to hike early in the day and carry plenty of water.

FINDING THE TRAILHEAD: From Highway 62 in Twentynine Palms, drive 13.7 miles south and west on Utah Trail/Park Boulevard to the east end of the Queen Valley Road. Turn right on this graded dirt road, and drive 1.3 miles to the Pine City Backcountry Board.

MAPS: Queen Mountain USGS.

THE HIKE: From the Pine City Trailhead, head north-northeast on the Pine City Trail. At 0.7 mile an old trail crosses at right angles; continue straight ahead another 0.7 mile to the site of Pine City. Despite its name, Pine City was at most a collection of a few shacks. The area has its own attractions, though, with scattered pines set amid granite boulders.

Desert Queen Mine

This easy 1.2-mile out-and-back hike takes you to the richest and most productive gold mine in the park. During the hot summer months, plan to hike early in the day and carry plenty of water. There is a dirt trailhead with restrooms.

FINDING THE TRAILHEAD: From Highway 62 in Twentynine Palms, drive 13.7 miles south and west on Utah Trail/Park Boulevard to the east end of the Queen Valley Road. Turn right on this graded dirt road, and drive 1.3 miles to the Pine City Backcountry Board.

MAPS: Queen Mountain USGS.

THE HIKE: From the Pine City Trailhead, head east on an easy trail. In less than 0.1 mile, a spur trail forks left and goes to a point overlooking the mine. Stay right and continue 1.1 miles to the mine area. The Queen Mine produced millions of dollars of gold—today the old mine shafts and some of the equipment dot the hillsides. A clue to the productiveness of such desert mines is the size of the tailings of waste rock removed from the mines. The size of the tailings at the Desert Queen Mine clearly show the size of the underground mine works.

Lucky Boy Vista

This easy 2.2-mile hike takes you to the Elton Mine and a viewpoint overlooking the Split Rock and Jumbo Rocks area. The out-and-back route begins at a dirt trailhead and permits horseback riding as well as hiking. During the hot summer months, plan to hike early in the day and carry plenty of water.

FINDING THE TRAILHEAD: From Highway 62 in Twentynine Palms, drive

13.7 miles south and west on Utah Trail/Park Boulevard to the east end of the Queen Valley Road. Turn right on this graded dirt road, and drive 0.9 mile to the Lucky Boy Vista parking area. This pull-out is 0.4 mile before reaching the Pine City Backcountry Board.

MAPS: Queen Mountain USGS.

THE HIKE: From the Lucky Boy Trailhead, head southeast on the Lucky Boy Trail. After 0.6 miles the trail crosses a wash marking the approximate halfway point. The trail ends at the mine, which is located on top of a bluff. The edge of the bluff offers views of the Split Rock area to the east and the Jumbo Rocks area to the south.

Crown Prince Lookout

This easy 2.6-mile out-and-back hike climbs to the summit of a small hill that is the site of a former observation tower. Horses share the trail with hikers. During the hot summer months, plan to hike early in the day and carry plenty of water. Parking and facilities are available at Jumbo Rocks Campground.

FINDING THE TRAILHEAD: From Highway 62 in Twentynine Palms, drive 11.9 miles south and west on Utah Trail/Park Boulevard to Jumbo Rocks Campground, on the left. Park at the entrance.

MAPS: Queen Mountain USGS.

THE HIKE: Since there is no parking where the Crown Prince Lookout Trail leaves Park Boulevard, park at the entrance to Jumbo Rocks Campground. Walk west on the paved road 0.3 mile, then turn left onto the Crown Prince Lookout Trail. Follow the trail 0.7 mile southeast to a fork. Turn right and follow the trail to its end on a small hill. Though lowly, this little hill will give you a sweeping view of the desert plain to the south and the piles of granite boulders around Jumbo Rocks Campground.

Skull Rock Nature Trail

This easy 1.5-mile interpretive nature trail loops past one of the park's most famous and frequently photographed landmarks, Skull Rock. Since the trail passes through Jumbo Rocks Campground, the loop can also be started there.

FINDING THE TRAILHEAD: From Highway 62 in Twentynine Palms, drive 11.6 miles south and west on Utah Trail/Park Boulevard to the Skull Rock Trailhead, just before reaching Jumbo Rocks Campground.

MAPS: Queen Mountain, Malapai Hill USGS.

THE HIKE: From the Skull Rock Trailhead, start on the south side of Park Boulevard and follow the Skull Rock Nature Trail southwest. Skull Rock is on the left, close to the road. The two "eye sockets" on the face of this granite boulder were carved from the rock through a combination of water running down the surface and wind removing the loose particles.

The trail continues southwest through a fantastic landscape of granite domes and boulders. Signs explain the geology and natural history along the way. When the trail appears to end in Jumbo Rocks Campground, turn right along the paved access road and walk a short distance to the campground entrance. Here you can pick up the trail on the north side of Park Boulevard. Now the trail heads northeast, parallel to the road, for a few hundred yards before wandering away to the north. When the trail turns east, it soon reaches the Skull Rock Trailhead.

Ivanpah Tank

This is a short, easy walk to a stock tank, or pond, which was built to water cattle when the area was used for ranching. The 0.9-mile loop starts from the Live Oak Picnic Area.

FINDING THE TRAILHEAD: From Highway 62 in Twentynine Palms, drive 10.8 miles south and west on Utah Trail/Park Boulevard to the Split Rock/Live Oak intersection. Turn left on the dirt road to the Live Oak Picnic Area, drive 0.1 mile to the fork in the road, and park.

MAPS: Queen Mountain, Malapai Hill USGS.

Ivanpah Tank was built by ranchers around 1900, and it still holds water.

THE HIKE: From the fork in the road, walk the right fork 0.2 mile through the picnic area to the road's end at a turnaround loop. Now walk south into the wash below the road and downstream about 100 yards to the huge oak tree growing in the wash. This live, or evergreen, oak is one of the largest in the park.

To reach Ivanpah Tank, continue down the wash to the southeast and then east. The tank is formed by a small concrete dam and holds water for a short time after the winter rains. Return to your vehicle by following an old road north toward the right side of the boulder pile. In 0.2 mile you'll reach the end of a road: Follow it 0.1 mile north to the road fork at the picnic area.

North Entrance Area

Pinto Wye Arrastra

This moderately strenuous cross-country loop hike to a historic mining artifact is 1.6 miles long. During the hot summer months, plan to hike early in the day and carry plenty of water.

> **FINDING THE TRAILHEAD:** From Highway 62 in Twentynine Palms, drive 8 miles south on Utah Trail/Park Boulevard and park at the small dirt pull-out on the left.
>
> **MAPS:** Queen Mountain USGS.

THE HIKE: From the small pull-out, cross the road and walk west into a ravine. Work your way up this ravine to the broad saddle at the top. Leave the saddle and head directly west, diagonally down the slope toward a wash that runs north. Aim for the point where the wash enters a jumble of granite boulders, and you'll spot the arrastra on the slopes east of the wash.

Arrastras were used to grind rock ore into fragments that could be further processed. The arrastra wheel was turned by mules, horses, burros, or sometimes the miners themselves. This arrastra is unusual in that it was built around a wagon wheel.

You can optionally return the way you came, for an easy hike of just 1 mile. However, the loop hike is an interesting and not-too-difficult way to finish. To continue, drop west into the wash below the arrastra, then follow the wash north. Soon the wash starts to wind its way through giant fallen boulders, and you'll need some scrambling skills to continue on down. Shortly the wash opens out into the desert flats. Stay right along the base of the hills to reach Park Boulevard. Follow the road 0.2 mile south back to the small pull-out and your vehicle.

Pleasant Valley Area

Malapai Hill

This easy 2.4-mile out-and-back hike leads cross-country to an isolated hill that offers a good view of the southern portion of the park. During the hot summer months, plan to hike early in the day and carry plenty of water.

FINDING THE TRAILHEAD: From Highway 62 in Twentynine Palms, drive 13.7 miles south and west on Utah Trail/Park Boulevard to the Geology Tour Road and turn left. Follow this four-wheel-drive road 4.7 miles south to the Squaw Tank pull-out on the Geology Tour.

MAPS: Malapai Hill USGS.

THE HIKE: From the pull-out at Stop #7, walk west across the desert flat to the base of the hill, then continue up the east slopes to the summit. From here, you can see the Queen Valley to the north, portions of Pleasant Valley to the southeast, and Lost Horse Mountain to the west. Malapai Hill is a volcanic dome (*malapai* means badlands or bad country in Paiute). There is an example of columnar jointing on the cliff below the summit to the northwest. Columnar joint occurs when a lava flow hardens slowly into basalt rock, and cracks part into vertical, six-sided columns as it cools and contracts.

Pinto Basin Area

Twin Tanks

An easy cross-country hike to a pair of small dams and ponds dating from the cattle-ranching days, this out-and-back route is 1.6 miles long.

FINDING THE TRAILHEAD: From Highway 62 in Twentynine Palms, drive 8.6 miles south on Utah Trail/Park Boulevard to Pinto Wye, then turn left on Pinto Basin Road. Continue south 2.4 miles to the Twin Tanks Trailhead and Backcountry Board, on the right, and park.

MAPS: Malapai Hill USGS.

THE HIKE: The Twin Tanks Trailhead is on the California Riding and Hiking Trail, which crosses the road and heads southwest. However, the route to Twin Tanks is cross-country, so head west across the desert flat, aiming for the mass of granite boulders directly west. If you bear just slightly left of the direct route, you'll drop into a broad wash less than halfway to the tanks. You can then follow the main bed wash directly to Twin Tanks. A key landmark is a 4-foot-high outcrop of white quartz next to Twin Tanks.

The two small dams are about 100 yards west, and northwest, respectively, from the quartz outcrop. Ranchers built the dams to catch runoff water for their stock.

Arch Rock Nature Trail

Comprised of a 0.3-mile nature trail in White Tank Campground that leads to a rare granite arch, this is an easy loop hike. Parking and facilities are available at White Tank Campground.

FINDING THE TRAILHEAD: From Highway 62 in Twentynine Palms, drive 8.6 miles south on Utah Trail/Park Boulevard to Pinto Wye, then turn left on Pinto Basin Road. Continue south 3.1 miles to White Tank Campground and turn left. There is day-use parking at site #9.

MAPS: Malapai Hill USGS.

THE HIKE: As with the other nature trails in the park, interpretive signs explain the natural history of the area, but on this trail the signs offer an especially good lesson in geology. The highlight of this short loop is the small natural arch in the granite. Natural arches, unlike natural bridges, do not span stream courses and do not have the powerful erosive effect of a stream to aid in their formation. Instead, a natural arch forms from a thin fin of rock by slow chemical weathering of each side. Since granite tends to weather into rounded domes and boulders rather than fins, natural arches are fairly rare in granite.

Cholla Garden Nature Trail

This easy interpretive nature trail passes through a remarkably dense patch of Bigelow, or teddy-bear, cholla cactus. Starting from and ending at a dirt parking lot, it's a 0.2-mile loop hike.

FINDING THE TRAILHEAD: From Highway 62 in Twentynine Palms, drive 8.6 miles south on Utah Trail/Park Boulevard to Pinto Wye, then turn left on Pinto Basin Road. Continue south 9.8 miles and park at a small pull-out on the right.

MAPS: Fried Liver Wash USGS.

THE HIKE: This short trail loops through a dense patch of Bigelow cholla, one of the characteristic plants of the Sonoran Desert in the eastern portion of the park. Though it looks cuddly, as the alternate name "teddy-bear cholla" suggests, this cactus is anything but. The stems and joints are covered with hundreds of razor-sharp spines, each tipped with microscopic barbs. If an animal or human is unfortunate enough to brush up against the cholla, the spines cling

The Cholla Garden Nature Trail passes through a remarkable concentration of teddy bear cholla in Pinto Basin.

fiercely to skin, clothing, or fur. Since the ends of the stems break off easily, the resulting cholla balls are transported to new locations by animals, where if conditions are favorable, a new plant will germinate.

The short trail also offers open views of Pinto Basin and the surrounding Hexie and Pinto Mountains.

Pinto Basin Sand Dunes

This easy 2.4-mile out-and-back cross-country walk takes you to a unique area of windblown sand in the vast expanses of Pinto Basin. During the hot summer months, plan to hike early in the day and carry plenty of water.

FINDING THE TRAILHEAD: From I–10 at the Pinto Basin Road exit, drive north 20.6 miles to the Turkey Flats Trailhead and Backcountry Board, on the right, and park.

MAPS: Pinto Mountain USGS.

THE HIKE: From the trailhead, walk northeast, cross-country, to the low sand dunes in the floor of the valley, about a mile away. Although the dunes themselves are not spectacular, the setting is. You may find it easier to appreciate the vast scale of the Sonoran Desert from the top of one of the low dunes, surrounded by hundreds of square miles of empty desert valley, limited only by the distant skyline of surrounding mountains. If winter rains have been plentiful, the valley floor may be a riot of wildflowers in the spring. The dunes themselves are well anchored by vegetation and do not appear to be actively migrating. Dunes such as these form when desert winds pick up loose sand, often from dried-up ice-age lakebeds, and pile it up in favorable areas. Return by hiking toward the highest point in the Hexie Mountains to the southwest, which will keep you on course for the trailhead.

Cottonwood Basin Area

Eagle Mountains Trail

This long day or overnight hike heads around to an old well and seasonal spring on the north side of the Eagle Mountains, following an unmaintained trail. It's a strenuous 13-mile out-and-back hike. During the hot summer months, plan to hike early in the day and carry plenty of water. The Cottonwood Visitor

Center, Campground, and Picnic Area are nearby.

FINDING THE TRAILHEAD: From I–10 at the Pinto Basin Road exit, drive north 7 miles to the Cottonwood Visitor Center and turn right. Drive 1.1 miles to the end of the road at Cottonwood Spring Backcountry Board and Trailhead. (You can also access the trail from the Cottonwood Group Campground.)

MAPS: Cottonwood Spring, Porcupine Wash, Conejo Well USGS.

THE HIKE: From the Cottonwood Spring Trailhead, walk a few yards west up the road to the Cottonwood Spring Nature Trail. Hike 0.4 mile to the Mastodon Peak Trail, and stay left on the Cottonwood Spring Nature Trail. When the nature trail ends at the Cottonwood Campground, walk the access road to the Eagle Mountains Trail at the back of the loop.

Follow the Eagle Mountain Trail, an old road, northeast across the gently sloping Sonoran Desert plain. In about 3 miles the trail passes through a broad pass in the northwestern Eagle Mountains, then turns east and descends a wide valley. Beyond the mouth of the valley, the trail skirts the northern foothills of the Eagle Mountains. About 1.9 miles from the broad pass, you'll meet the side trail to Conejo Well. Turn right here and hike another 0.8 mile south up a canyon to Conejo Well. There is a seasonal spring just above the dry well.

Mastodon Peak Loop

This 2.2-mile easy loop hike combines part of the Cottonwood Spring Nature Trail with a trail past Mastodon Peak and Cottonwood Spring Oasis. The Cottonwood Visitor Center, Campground, and Picnic Area are nearby.

FINDING THE TRAILHEAD: From I–10 at the Pinto Basin Road exit, drive north 7 miles to the Cottonwood Visitor Center and turn right. Drive 1.1 miles to the end of the road at Cottonwood Spring Backcountry Board and Trailhead. (You can also access the trail from the Cottonwood Group Campground.)

MAPS: Cottonwood Spring USGS.

THE HIKE: From the Cottonwood Spring Trailhead, walk a few yards west up the road to the Cottonwood Spring Nature Trail. Walk this trail northwest and north up a wash to the Mastodon Peak Trail. Informative signs on the nature

Cottonwood Spring Oasis was an essential watering place during the pioneer days.

trail explain the native Cahuilla tribe's use of Sonoran Desert plants for medicine, food, and tools and materials.

Turn right onto the Mastodon Peak Trail, which immediately passes the site of the old Winona Mill. Little remains of the mill except concrete foundations. Built by George Hulsey in the 1920s, the mill was used to crush ore from the Mastodon Mine as well as claims in the Dale Mining District to the north. Hulsey and other residents planted non-native trees and shrubs, which still grow in the mill area.

The trail heads northeast and climbs up to the Mastodon Mine, just below the top of Mastodon Peak. A slanting mine shaft, sealed with a locked grate, and some mining machinery mark the spot. Hulsey operated the mine from 1919 to 1932, and its gold ore was assayed at $744 per ton. Unfortunately, the miners, following the main gold vein, eventually discovered that the rich ore ended at a fault, and the mine was abandoned.

From just south of the mine, it is possible to make the short scramble to the top of Mastodon Peak, an optional side hike that adds only 0.1 mile to the hike. For such an easy-to-reach summit, the views are outstanding, including the southern portions of the park, as well as the Coachella Valley and Salton Sea to the south.

The trail now descends south into a wash, where it meets the Lost Palms Trail. Turn right and follow the Lost Palms Trail northwest to Cottonwood Spring, marked by a stand of California fan palms. Between 1870 and 1910 the spring was a critical watering point in the otherwise arid desert. Because it was one of only two watering places between Mecca and the Dale Mining District, Cottonwood Spring was a popular and necessary stopping point for freight haulers, prospectors, and other desert travelers. These travelers planted the California fan palms and Fremont cottonwoods that shade the canyon bottom. For a time, water was pumped 18 miles from the spring to the Iron Chief Mine in the Eagle Mountains.

Bedrock mortars, marked by a sign, are the only remaining evidence that natives used Cottonwood Spring for centuries before white people came. These small basins in the rock were carved out by the grinding of grain and seeds with a rounded stone called a pestle.

Output from the spring has varied widely. Around 1900 the spring apparently delivered around 3,000 gallons per day, but by 1970 the flow had dropped to a few gallons per day. There is evidence that earthquakes and fault activity influence springs in the desert, and this is borne out by the 1971 San Fernando Valley earthquake. After the earthquake the output of Cottonwood Spring increased somewhat, to about 30 gallons per day.

From the spring, walk less than 0.1 mile west to the trailhead.

Moortens Mill Site

An easy 1.2 miles out and back, this cross-country hike follows the route of a historic teamsters' road to an old stamp-mill site. The Cottonwood Visitor Center, Campground, and Picnic Area are nearby.

FINDING THE TRAILHEAD: From I–10 at the Pinto Basin Road exit, drive north 7 miles to the Cottonwood Visitor Center and turn right. Drive 1.1 miles to the end of the road at Cottonwood Spring Trailhead and Backcountry Board.

MAPS: Cottonwood Spring USGS.

THE HIKE: From the Cottonwood Spring Trailhead, walk less than 0.1 mile east down to Cottonwood Spring, then turn right and walk south down the wash below the spring. Although this route was routinely traveled by heavy freight wagons at the end of the nineteenth century, little trace of the old road remains, except at Chilcoot Pass where a bypass was constructed on the right side of the wash to avoid the boulder-choked canyon bottom.

Palo verde, mesquite, and desert willow, commonly found along washes in the Sonoran Desert, grow along this wash as well.

Just 0.6 mile down the wash, you'll encounter the scanty remains of Moortens Mill, which was used to crush mined gold ore for further processing. "Cactus" Slim Moorten built the five-stamp mill in the early 1930s to process gold-bearing rocks mined from his three claims in the area. He abandoned the operation in 1939.

Lost Palms Oasis

This moderate 6.6-mile out-and-back hike leads to one of the largest palm oases in the park. Lost Palms Canyon, at the end of the hike, is in a day-use area. During the hot summer months, plan to hike early in the day and carry plenty of water. The Cottonwood Visitor Center, Campground, and Picnic Area are nearby.

FINDING THE TRAILHEAD: From I–10 at the Pinto Basin Road exit, drive north 7 miles to the Cottonwood Visitor Center and turn right. Drive 1.1 miles to the end of the road at Cottonwood Spring Backcountry Board and Trailhead.

MAPS: Cottonwood Spring USGS.

THE HIKE: From the Cottonwood Spring Trailhead, walk less than 0.1 mile east down to Cottonwood Spring, then continue east-southeast on the Lost Palms Trail. At 0.7 mile the Mastodon Peak Trail comes in from the left; stay right and continue east-southeast on the Lost Palms Trail.

The trail works its way through the foothills of the Eagle Mountains, crossing what seems to be an endless series of washes and low ridges, before dropping down to an overlook above Lost Palms Oasis. More than one hundred palms grace this spring and attract numerous birds and other animals, including bighorn sheep. Bighorn sheep require large expanses of rugged desert mountains in order to survive. Their presence is one of the major reasons for the designation of day-use areas in the park. Though these hardy animals can go for days without water, they do require water to survive. In the park, day-use areas protect areas with springs, rock tanks, and other seasonal water sources. Your best chance to spot one of these reclusive animals is to sit quietly at an overlook, such as this one, and scan the rocky hillside.

Appendix A:
For More Information

Cunningham, Bill, and Polly Burke. *Best Easy Day Hikes Joshua Tree.* Guilford, Conn.: The Globe Pequot Press, 2000.

Decker, Barbara, and Robert Decker. *Road Guide to Joshua Tree National Park.* Mariposa, Calif.: Double Decker Press, 1999.

Grubbs, Bruce. *Desert Hiking Tips.* Helena, Mont.: Falcon Publishing, 1999.

———. *Desert Sense.* Seattle: Mountaineers Books, 2005.

Pasachoff, Jay M. *Field Guide to Stars and Planets.* Boston: Houghton Mifflin, 1999.

Trent, D. D., and Richard W. Hazlett. *Joshua Tree National Park Geology.* Twentynine Palms, Calif.: Joshua Tree National Park Association, 2002.

Vogel, Randy. *Rock Climbing Joshua Tree.* Guilford, Conn.: The Globe Pequot Press, 1992.

———. *Rock Climbing Joshua Tree West.* Guilford, Conn.: The Globe Pequot Press, 2006.

Appendix B: Resources

Big Morongo Canyon Preserve
PO Box 780
Morongo Valley, CA 92256
(760) 363–7190
www.bigmorongo.org

Joshua Tree National Park
74485 National Park Drive
Twentynine Palms, CA 92277
(760) 367–5500
www.nps.gov/jotr

Joshua Tree National Park Association
Joshua Tree National Park
74485 National Park Drive
Twentynine Palms, CA 92277
(760) 367–5525
www.joshuatree.org

Bureau of Land Management
Palm Springs–South Coast Resource Area
690 West Garnet Avenue
North Palm Springs, CA 92258
(760) 251–4800
www.blm.gov/ca/palmsprings/directory.html

Bruce Grubbs is an avid hiker, mountain biker, paddler, and cross-country skier who has been exploring the American West for more than thirty-five years. An active outdoor writer and photographer, he's written eighteen outdoor guidebooks, and his photographs have been published in *Backpacker* and other magazines. An active charter pilot, he currently lives in Flagstaff, Arizona.

Other FalconGuide by Bruce Grubbs:

A FalconGuide to Saguaro National Park

Basic Essentials: Using GPS

Best Easy Day Hikes Flagstaff

Best Easy Day Hikes Sedona

Camping Arizona

Desert Hiking Tips

Explore! Shasta Country

Hiking Arizona

Hiking Arizona's Superstition and Mazatzal Country

Hiking Great Basin National Park

Hiking Nevada

Hiking Northern Arizona

Hiking Oregon's Central Cascades

Mountain Biking Flagstaff and Sedona

Mountain Biking Phoenix

Mountain Biking St. George and Cedar City

For more information, check the author's Web site at www.brucegrubbs.com.